The Courage of Their Convictions

Stories of Inspirational Men
and Women of Faith

Gemma Grant

VERITAS

Published 2021 by
Veritas Publications
7–8 Lower Abbey Street
Dublin 1, Ireland

publications@veritas.ie
www.veritas.ie

ISBN 978 1 80097 007 6

10 9 8 7 6 5 4 3 2 1

Cover images: *Monsignor Hugh O'Flaherty*, mural in Killarney, Ireland, © Dmol, commons.wikimedia.org/wiki/File:Mural_of_Monsignor_Hugh_O'Flaherty_in_Killarney,_Ireland.jpg; *Sister Clare Crockett*, mural in Derry City, © Rowaves, commons. wikimedia.org/wiki/File:Clare_Crockett_mural.png; *Frank Duff*, © Legion of Mary; *Little Nellie of Holy God*; *Father Patrick Peyton*; *Saint Brigid*.

A catalogue record for this book is available from the British Library.

Typeset by Padraig McCormack
Printed in Ireland by SPRINT-print Ltd, Dublin

Veritas books are printed on paper made from the wood pulp of managed forests. For every tree felled, at least one tree is planted, thereby renewing natural resources.

Contents

Introduction

This collection of stories details the enormous contribution made by male and female religious and laity to the world. Through evangelisation, good example and tremendous personal courage, their efforts have marked many of them out for sainthood.

From humble beginnings in a troubled Italian American home, Mother Angelica went on to establish EWTN – a global network that began life in the garage of her convent. Her continued battles with bishops and cardinals for control of the network led her to inform one bishop in true Sicilian fashion: 'I'll blow the darn thing up before you get your hands on it!'

Pope Pius XII, erroneously referred to as 'Hitler's Pope', is depicted here in a very different light. While criticised for not speaking out more against Nazi atrocities during

World War II, behind the scenes he was working with the allies and helping to save the lives of countless Jews.

Hollywood actress Dolores Hart gave Elvis his first onscreen kiss. While still in her twenties, and with a promising acting career ahead of her, Dolores turned her back on Hollywood to become a Benedictine nun.

Closer to home, Fr Hugh O'Flaherty, known as 'The Scarlet Pimpernel of the Vatican', founded the Rome Escape Line. His organisation saved countless Jews and allies from Nazi oppression. He even managed to convert his one-time nemesis, Herbert Kappler – head of Rome's notorious Gestapo.

Sister Blandina earned the title 'The Fastest Nun in the West'. While attempting to set up schools and hospitals in the American Wild West of the 1800s, she struck up an unlikely friendship with a notorious outlaw.

Archbishop Fulton J. Sheen was television's first Catholic evangelist. His political astuteness and prophetic vision warned of the dangers of the Red Peril – Russia – at a time when America looked on Russia as an ally against German fascism. His keen insight brought him to the attention of the FBI, who opened a file on him and closely followed his political comments.

Dorothy Day was considered one of the most remarkable American women and social reformers of the twentieth century. Dorothy went from Marxist revolutionary to Catholic social reformer.

Many of the people discussed in this book have inspired films, TV series, books and plays. Jesuit priests who performed an exorcism on a young boy in America in 1949 could scarcely imagine their work would inspire one of the most revered horror movies of all time: *The Exorcist.*

As soldiers of Christ, these brave men and women took up their cross to overcome insurmountable obstacles, inspiring many followers and making their lives worth remembering.

MALE
RELIGIOUS

Pope Pius XII

Hitler's Pope?

> A Vicar of Christ who sees these things before his
> eyes and still remains silent because of state policies,
> who delays even one day ... such a pope ... is a
> criminal.

These are the words of Fr Fontana, the young Jesuit
protagonist in Rolf Hochhuth's play, *The Representative.*
The play destroyed the good name and character of
Pope Pius XII. First performed in Berlin in 1963 and later
that year in London, it was avidly received. Although
Hochhuth was a young boy during the Nazi occupation of
Rome, his critique led many writers, historians and literati
to severely criticise the papacy. The criticism contained

and expounded upon within *The Representative* led to the welcomed publication of John Cornwell's book, *Hitler's Pope*, some thirty years later. However, one reviewer of the book, Kevin Madigan, claimed that it was 'highly dependent in many of its chapters on already-published secondary literature'.[1] Despite *Hitler's Pope* presenting more anti-Catholic sentiments than historical facts, it resulted in renewed criticism of Pope Pius XII and the Vatican, practically accusing it of being solely responsible for the Holocaust. Pope Pius XII was described by one Jewish critic as being cold, aloof and removed from the real world. Even the German Ambassador to the Holy See commented on the fact that Pius seemed more interested in preserving Vatican neutrality than denouncing the deportation of Jews.

However, under closer scrutiny, a vastly different picture emerges. A diverse plethora of historical documents have been carefully studied, revealing a humanitarian pontiff who walked a tightrope over turbulent waters that threatened to drown not only Jewry, but any country that stood in its way. No mere pope could hinder Hitler's desires to conquer Europe or thwart plans for the Final Solution – Jewish extermination. Nazi occupation of Rome in 1943 resulted in a demarcation line being painted around the Vatican to remind the pope where his tenuous power ended. With diplomatic skill, Pius carried out one of the most difficult poker moves in history: winning with a losing hand.

Léon Poliakov, a French historian of Russian-Jewish lineage, verified that Pius hid Jews in convents, churches and in his summer residence, Castel Gandolfo. Poliakov was in no doubt that Pius issued secret instructions urging Churches in Europe to intervene discretely on behalf of the Jews. It is widely acknowledged that in his role as Archbishop of Istanbul at the time, Pope John XXIII rescued thousands of Jews. This, he confirmed, was done on explicit orders from Pope Pius XII.

Pius was castigated for not publicly speaking out against Nazi activities. However, those who took a direct stand against Hitler paid a heavy price. In reprisal for a partisan attack on German police in Rome 1944, over three hundred and thirty men and boys were indiscriminately rounded up and massacred in the Ardeatine Caves in Rome. Two years previous, Reinhard Heydrich, second only to Heinrich Himmler and leading architect of the Final Solution, was murdered in Prague by Czech partisans. Reprisals were swift and brutal. One estimate claims that five thousand Czechs were murdered in retaliation. The dead included Jews and priests. Two entire villages, considered complicit, were wiped out.

Hitler initially wanted to purge the population of Prague, adding weight to the adage 'resistance is futile'. This was the world Pius presided over as head of the universal Church: a world of mass killings and savagery never before witnessed in the annals of man.

This was, for many, the age of the Antichrist. This was an evil even the pope could not evade. Pius acted as a go-between for German generals opposed to Hitler. He conveyed their plans for a revolt against Hitler to the British Foreign Office. Due to terms and conditions not being met by both sides, the offensive never materialised. The pope informed Sir D'Arcy Osborne, British Minister to the Holy See, that any hopes for a settlement were dashed. Had this dangerous course of action been successful, it would have done more to end the war than publicly speaking out. If news of it leaked out at the time, the entire Vatican staff – including the pope – would have suffered the same fate as the citizens of Prague. A senior British official informed the pope's secretary, Fr Leiber SJ, that, in his quest for peace, Pius went to the outer limits of what was possible for a pope.

In 1943, Pius wrote to the College of Cardinals urging caution when making public denouncements for fear of worsening matters. Many Jews approved of this approach. One Jewish couple, the Wolfssons, were sheltered in a convent in Rome run by German nuns. Pius arranged for them to escape to Spain. Years later, as they spoke of those terrifying days, the couple endorsed the need for silence. They claimed that none of the Jews they knew wanted the pope to take an open stand as they were all living in fear of discovery. They preferred to remain hidden until a means of escape could be arranged. They knew that if the pope protested, the Gestapo would have intensified efforts to hunt them down. The Wolfssons stated that many Jews were of that opinion both then and now.

Perhaps the last testimonies in this chapter should be from those who lived through the horror, rather than with pseudo-historians who write with prejudiced hindsight from the comfort of their drawing rooms. While the exact figure may never be known, one Jewish historian, Emilio Pinchas Lapide, believes that the Catholic Church saved as many as 850,000 Jews from the death camps. He stated Pope Pius XII saved more lives than all government or international agencies combined. Another writer, David Herstig, estimated that 360,000 Romanian Jews living in Israel owe their lives to Pope Pius XII.

Possibly one of the greatest tributes comes from Israel Zolli, chief rabbi of Rome from 1940 to 1945. The rabbi spoke of his time in hiding and had nothing but the greatest regard for Pope Pius XII, the clergy and the

Italian people who took Jews and escaped prisoners of war (POWs) into their monasteries and homes. Zoller claims that of the eight thousand Jewish residents of Rome, some seven thousand were saved by going into hiding. He also testifies that nuns slept in the basements of their convents, having turned their beds over to Jewish refugees. He experienced first-hand the pope's personal involvement in providing the shortfall of gold bullion demanded from the Jews by the Nazis, on the pretext that they would not face deportation. This was a promise the Nazis readily broke. The rabbi and published author converted to Catholicism in 1945. He was christened Eugenio Maria, in homage to Pope Pius XII who was born Eugenio Maria Giuseppe Pacelli. When Pope Pius XII died in 1958, the Israeli Prime Minister, Golda Meir, paid tribute to him at the United Nations.

The Jewish tributes to Pope Pius XII contrasted sharply with the jaundiced views propagated by his detractors. The pope accused of indifference and criminal activity in Hochhuth's play was a pope Hochhuth never knew. Israel Zolli, who actually knew the pope, said of him: 'No one asks for anything except to follow in the footsteps of the Master under the guidance of Pius XII.'[2]

Father Edward Joseph Flanagan

Founder of Boys Town

'There's no such thing as a bad boy,' stated Spencer Tracey in his Academy Award-winning role as Fr Edward Flanagan in the 1938 movie *Boys Town*. The film, based on the real life of Fr Flanagan, featured a young Mickey Rooney playing the cocky protagonist, Whitey Marsh. The movie raised awareness of the plight of homeless children in America and brought to greater prominence the sterling work of Irish-born priest, Fr Edward Flanagan.

Unlike those he cared for, Fr Flanagan came from a stable background. He was the eighth of eleven children born to John and Nora Flanagan. On his birth in 1886 in the village of Ballymoe, Co. Roscommon, Edward was possibly premature and considered very delicate. Fearing he would not survive, his grandfather Patrick wrapped him in a blanket, nursing him for hours in front of the fire. Edward survived but struggled with poor health throughout his life. In a letter to a friend, he light-heartedly described himself as the delicate little shepherd boy who was good for nothing but caring for the sheep. This turned out to be excellent training for when he would care for the homeless flock of America. His upbringing of family rosaries and honest, hard work formed the character of the young boy. His father's stories of the Irish struggle for independence and heroic tales of patriots and saints found willing ears in Edward. It was from St Benedict that Fr Flanagan took his rule of life: 'pray and work.'

In 1904, along with his sister Nellie, he travelled to New York and began his studies for the priesthood. However, double pneumonia halted his studies for a year. To recuperate, he made his way to Omaha to stay with his brother, Fr Patrick. Nellie, who was Fr Patrick's housekeeper, nursed her younger brother back to health. Due to recurring health problems, it would be eight years before he was ordained to the priesthood in Austria in 1912.

One of his first assignments on returning to America led him down a path of social reform. On Easter Sunday

1913, Omaha suffered a devastating tornado that destroyed one-third of the city and left 155 people dead and hundreds more homeless. Appointed to St Patrick's Church, Fr Flanagan helped the mortician retrieve dead bodies and arranged for their burials. For the next two years, he provided for the homeless and jobless. Receiving permission from the bishop, he opened the derelict Burlington Hotel, which went on to house fifty-seven men. Due to growing numbers, he secured the larger premises of The Working Men's Hotel, which sheltered up to one thousand men. With America's entry into World War I in 1917, Fr Flanagan's hotel emptied out as many of the men enlisted. However, news of the hotel had spread and their places were taken by new drifters who all had one thing in common – unstable backgrounds. One of the homeless men told Fr Flanagan that growing up he had wanted to be an architect, but his difficult upbringing prevented it. The man suggested to Fr Flanagan that he help young people to make something better of their lives.

Father Flanagan studied the juvenile justice system of the time. He became so knowledgeable that he was often consulted by judges on these matters. Many of the boys were paroled to him, thereby avoiding the harsh reform schools where corporal punishment reigned. Towards the end of 1917, he opened his first shelter for boys in Omaha.

With help from the Notre Dame Sisters and well-trained teachers, a school was established for one hundred and fifty boys.

By 1921, Fr Flanagan had secured the deed to Overlook Farm on the outskirts of Omaha, which later developed into Boys Town. A devotee of the rosary, he encouraged the boys – who came from different ethnic and religious backgrounds – to pray. He told them: 'Every boy should pray; how he prays is up to him.' Each boy attended weekly religious services. One of the many virtues Fr Flanagan instilled in the boys was building character. He firmly believed that no boy could reach his full potential without a strong, honest character. He encouraged them to respect authority and help each other. In 1943, the Boys Town advertisement depicted a boy carrying a younger boy on his back, with the caption: 'He ain't heavy, Father ... he's m'brother!' As a counsellor, Fr Flanagan spoke out vehemently against corporal punishment and reprimanded adults for not encouraging children. During many of his radio broadcasts, which began in 1926, he reminded his listeners: 'When you help a child today, you write the history of tomorrow.' He encouraged listeners to pass on Christian values to their children.

The original Boys Town was akin to a town within a town, where boys ruled without fences or fear of corporal punishment. They elected their own government and mayor. Education and guidance motivated the boys, helping to shape them into responsible citizens. Alongside this, they formed their own choir and participated in athletic events – they were the first in America to have a racially integrated sports team. By 1934, they had their own post office and fire station.

In 1946, Fr Flanagan visited Ireland and was fiercely critical of conditions within the prisons, industrial schools and youth care facilities, calling them 'a disgrace to the nation'. During World War II, the War Office named him 'America's No. 1 War Dad', due to the number of servicemen who named him their next of kin. In 1947, Fr Flanagan toured Asia to investigate the need for aid for war orphans. His findings were later presented to President Truman at a White House meeting. Many distinguished visitors passed through the gates of Boys Town. Mother Teresa, Nancy Regan and Laura Bush were grateful recipients of the Fr Flanagan Award for Service to Youth. In 1962, the Boys Town Choir recorded a Christmas album with the Everly Brothers.

Before his death in 1948, the widely travelled priest cared for some six thousand youths. Eighty-nine global programmes are attributed to his example. Boys Town expanded to include girls and, in 1991, they elected their first female mayor. Today, Boys Town provides care to some 1.4 million families annually. Of the many honours Fr Flanagan received, his greatest is the cause for his beatification, opened on 17 March 2012 in the Archdiocese of Omaha. The Father Flanagan League, initiated by the alumni of Boys Town, aims to educate and inform people of the sanctity of the life of their founder. Its desire is to spread worldwide devotion of his example as a protector of youth and to encourage pilgrimages to where he now rests in Boys Town, Nebraska. He did so much for his boys that it was never forgotten. In return, they pray for his canonisation, proving Fr Flanagan correct when he said of them: 'There's no such thing as a bad boy.'

Father James Keller

Founder of The Christophers

As six-year-old James Keller sat in his classroom, he listened as a young priest told the class that one day one of them may become a priest and help the world. While the young boy didn't fully understand what the priest meant, in his autobiography, *To Light a Candle*, he distinctly remembered hiding under his desk, hoping the priest wasn't referring to him. It would be some twenty years later before Fr James Keller became that priest that indeed helped the world by establishing The Christophers, a lay Catholic organisation that would spread the light of Christ throughout the world.

James Keller was born in California in 1900. He was one of six children to Irish immigrant parents. His mother was Portuguese on her father's side. His father, James, changed the family name from Kelleher to Keller to avoid anti-Irish sentiment. The household was described as devoutly Catholic.

In 1921, the young James joined the Catholic Mission Society of America, now known as Maryknoll, a training ground for young missionaries established in 1911 in New York. Unlike his fellow priests, James didn't get to travel overseas as he would have liked. Instead, he spent his priesthood promoting the work of Maryknoll throughout California, the Midwest and New York. He firmly believed that the light of Christ in just one person was enough to spark global renewal and lead the world out of the darkness of world wars and destructive ideologies. Father Keller believed that God has given each individual a special task in life that belongs to no one else.

During the 1930s he travelled extensively throughout the country promoting the work of the Maryknoll missionary priests. From the various audiences who received him warmly, he asked for their prayers and finances to help the work of the missions. As he later recalled, it was during these talks that he pondered how his audience could play a missionary role themselves. In 1945 he founded The Christophers. The aim of the movement was to encourage people from every sphere of life to carry the Gospel message from their communities to the world in order to preserve the Judeo-Christian way of life. Father Keller envisaged the organisation as being informal, with no membership or fees. He preferred to focus attention on what one person could do to help their fellow man. He once gave the example of a lady who saved the job of a Black man working in a small filling station in an area of America where racial tensions were high. The owner of the station reluctantly had to let the Black employee go as customers refused to buy their gas at his station. The lady in question approached the owner and asked how many customers he had lost. When he told her, she offered to find him as many and more replacement customers. When she succeeded in her efforts, the Black man was re-employed at the gas station.

In 1946, a published article entitled, 'You Can Be a Christopher' appeared in *The Catholic World* magazine. Father Keller remembered that the launch of The Christophers was overwhelming. He claimed it was akin to dropping a pebble into a pool – the circles took on a life of their own as they widened outward and onward. He immediately began publishing a regular newsletter, *Christopher News Notes*, reaching a wider audience through media outlets and always bringing a message of hope to his readers and listeners.

Realising the importance of getting prominent people involved in bringing the light of Christ to the world, Fr Keller set about encouraging American politicians to promote Christian teaching to counteract what he saw as the destruction of America. 'As America goes, so goes the world,' he informed his followers. He adopted the Chinese proverb 'It is better to light one candle than to curse the darkness' for The Christophers. He concentrated his efforts on spreading word of the organisation to millions through the mediums of film and television. In 1952, he launched his first Christopher production, featuring many Hollywood legends. Bing Crosby, Jack Benny, Bob Hope, William Holden, Loretta Young and Ann Blyth all starred in the first of many weekly series. The central message of the shows was 'You Can Change the World', taken from his bestselling book of the same title published in 1948.

Father Keller spent his active ministry as a public figure, a radio and television personality, a writer and, most importantly, a religious leader and spiritual counsellor. Those who met him were left with little doubt about their own importance as individuals. To each and all he had but one message: 'You individually have a mission in life to fulfil, a special job to do. You can do something no other person can do to shape the world in which you live.'

In 1972, due to failing health, Fr Keller wrote:

> Since tomorrow, 15 August, is the forty-seventh anniversary of my ordination, it seems fitting to ponder more seriously than ever the fact that a relatively short time is left to me to prepare for my final summons. Throughout my life I have looked forward with joyful anticipation to the 'homecoming' day when I will meet my Saviour face to face. But the nearer I get to that glorious occasion, the more unworthy I feel. I find myself counting more than ever before on the mercy of the Lord to make up for my defects and shortcomings. Through prayer and good works during the time left, I can do penance for my imperfections and prove that I am truly sorry for any and all of my offences against a loving God.[3]

In 1976, Fr Keller received the Benemerenti Medal from Pope Paul VI in recognition of his fifty years' service to The Christophers and the Maryknoll Fathers. One year later, aged seventy-seven, Fr Keller died in a New York hospital. Today, Christopher radio and television programmes reach a weekly audience of over five million, and *Christopher News Notes* has over one million readers around the world. The annual Christopher Media Awards is some seventy years old, seeking those within the media who 'affirm the highest values of the human spirit'. The awards hope to encourage men, women and children to pursue excellence in creative areas that will positively influence a mass audience.

Father Keller lived to see the Christopher motto carried to the farthest ends of the earth: 'Better to light one candle than to curse the darkness.' Even after his death, the candle he lit continues to glow.

Monsignor Hugh O'Flaherty

The Scarlet Pimpernel of the Vatican

When Hugh O'Flaherty entered Mungret Jesuit College in Co. Limerick in 1918, the twenty-year-old Kerry man had his sights set on the missionary fields. The young seminarian moved quickly through the clerical ranks, attaining several doctorates, mastering numerous languages and becoming a Monsignor by the age of thirty-six. His skills were not overlooked by his superiors who earmarked him for the diplomatic office rather than missionary work. Accepting the challenge, Monsignor O'Flaherty served in various countries before returning to Rome in 1938 to become an official at the Holy Office. His diplomatic skills and missionary zeal, which never left him, would be put to good use the following year when Europe went to war.

In 1940, under the dictatorship of Benito Mussolini, Italy allied itself with Germany. Italian POW camps sprang up between 1940 and 1942, detaining some seventy-five thousand captured allied troops. Concerned for the well-being of the men, the Vatican assigned the Papal Nuncio, Francesco Duca, to inspect the camps along with Fr O'Flaherty, who acted as assistant and interpreter. Father O'Flaherty was no admirer of British imperialism. He witnessed the Black and Tan atrocities in Ireland and lost several friends during that period. He once told a colleague, 'I don't think there is anything to choose between Britain and Germany'. However, his genuine concern was for the allied prisoners. With great enthusiasm, he set about ensuring they received proper clothing, blankets and Red Cross packages. He also used Vatican Radio to pass messages from prisoners to their families. His protests over conditions in the camps were so vehement that the Italian authorities pressurised the Church to have him reassigned. However, their demands failed.

Father Hugh found another way to help the POWs that eventually led him into a dangerous game of cat and mouse with SS Lieutenant Colonel Herbert Kappler, one of Rome's most notorious Nazis. When Mussolini was overthrown in 1943, Italy signed an unconditional armistice with General Eisenhower. Thousands of POWs escaped and moved across Italy, and many received sanctuary from the Vatican. It fell to Kappler, as head of the Gestapo, to restore order to Rome, regardless of the cost to life or liberty. During the brutal nine months of Nazi occupation of Rome, Kappler oversaw the executions of over three hundred Italian citizens who were shot in the Ardeatine Caves in reprisal for a partisan attack. He also saw to the deportation of Rome's Jews to the concentration camps, even after having secured gold bullion on the false promise that it would safeguard the Jewish community. With papal approval, Fr O'Flaherty took a stand against Kappler and established what became known as the Rome Escape Line. His endeavours earned him the nickname 'The Scarlet Pimpernel of the Vatican'.

With the assistance of clergy and laity, Fr O'Flaherty provided safe houses, food, clothing and essential documents for Jews, POWs and dissenters. This underground movement, which was given a personal contribution from Pope Pius XII, even contributed to the gold bullion demanded by Kappler from the Jewish community. Colonel Kappler, exerting further authority, had a white demarcation line painted around the Vatican as a reminder to Pope Pius XII where Vatican authority ended. Such was the effectiveness of the Rome Escape

Line in thwarting Gestapo plans that Colonel Kappler ordered that Fr O'Flaherty be shot dead if he dared step over the line. Refusing to be intimidated, the Monsignor used various disguises to continue his work. On one occasion he dressed as a nun and walked across German lines unobserved. However, not all the clergy helping the Resistance managed to escape detection. Some were arrested and held in the notorious Regina Coeli prison where they were tortured and executed.

During his activities as founder of the Rome Escape Line, Fr Hugh and his associates managed to save over six thousand people from Nazi oppression and execution. By all accounts a quiet and unassuming man, his exploits are best remembered by those who served with him and by those whom he helped. In 1995, Franciscan Sister Noreen Dennehy gave evidence to a Jewish organisation that was researching this period of history. Sister Noreen knew Fr Hugh well and worked with him to hide persecuted Jews in the Franciscan convent. Sister spoke of how Fr Hugh risked his life on numerous occasions, helping to hide as many as fifteen Jews at any one time in the convent. Jewish survivors spoke of hiding in hospital beds pretending to be patients with contagious diseases. One young Jewish girl remembered being instructed to cough loudly when armed soldiers entered the wards.

This was a great deterrent, apparently. All of this, Sister said, was done with the implicit support of Pope Pius XII.

In 1963, the BBC decided to pay tribute to Monsignor O'Flaherty by featuring him on *This Is Your Life*. However, it is claimed that because of his poor health at the time, it was decided instead to dedicate the show to Sam Derry, the British officer who assisted Fr O'Flaherty in the Rome Escape Line.[4] One source claims that host Eamonn Andrews was outraged at the last-minute decision. However, Fr O'Flaherty made a surprise appearance at the end of the show, delighting guests and the estimated eight million viewers who tuned in to watch. Monsignor O'Flaherty was awarded the Congressional Medal of Freedom, given a CBE and named Notary of the Holy Office. He was the first Irishman to be hailed by Israel as 'Righteous Among the Nations'. His wartime escapades have been depicted by biographers and, in 1983, he was immortalised on the big screen by Gregory Peck in the film *The Scarlet and the Black*.

Father O'Flaherty retired to Cahersiveen in Co. Kerry and sadly passed away in 1963 at the age of sixty-five. In 2013, the Hugh O'Flaherty Memorial was unveiled in his hometown of Killarney. Three years later, Monsignor O'Flaherty was honoured again when a plaque, funded by the Irish Government, was erected within the Vatican walls. Some two hundred people attended the event, including family members, those involved in the Rome Escape Line, and ambassadors from Germany, USA, England and Canada. Members of the Hugh O'Flaherty Memorial Society were greeted by Pope Frances. What Fr O'Flaherty would have made of the accolades is difficult to gauge.

Apparently not a man to hold grudges, Fr O'Flaherty obliged in helping Herbert Kappler's wife and children escape before the allies took Rome. Kappler was sentenced to life in prison without parole following his trial in 1948. His only visitor was none other than Fr Hugh, who was asked by Colonel Kappler to visit him. Over a period of time, the two men became friends. Father Hugh saw a certain irony in his one-time foe, who wanted him dead at all costs, now forming a friendship with him. The once notorious Nazi described the Monsignor as a 'fatherly friend'. It is a firmly held belief that Fr O'Flaherty was not only Kappler's closest confidant but he also had the greatest influence on his spiritual development. Monsignor O'Flaherty received Herbert Kappler into the Catholic Church in 1959. He had advised Kappler to postpone his conversion until after his sentence, in case it looked like a conversion of convenience.

Perhaps the greatest achievement of Fr O'Flaherty, who had entered the Jesuit college in 1918 with the intention of becoming a missionary, was converting his nemesis into not only a friend but, conceivably, a repentant sinner.

Father Joseph Walijewski

A Pencil in God's Hand

One of nine children, Joseph Walijewski was born in Michigan in 1924 to poor Polish parents. At the age of eight he sold newspapers to help the family finances. His parents were devout Catholics and his mother had great devotion to St Joseph. She asked three things of the saint: first, that she would have a son who would enter the priesthood and who she would name Joseph; second, that her son would build a church and name it after St Joseph; finally, her third and last request was that she would die on the feast day of St Joseph. All three of her requests came to be. She lived to see her son enter the priesthood in 1950. Twenty-one years later, she died on 19 March 1971, the feast day of St Joseph.

Father Joseph Walijewski received Holy Orders in the Cathedral of St Joseph, Wisconsin. He saw the hand of God in his ordination as he freely admitted he was no academic. He was told twice that he did not have the intellect for the priesthood but he promised God if He helped him to become a priest, he would spend five years in the missions. The hierarchy said of him: 'Joe Walijewski may not be the most intelligent priest, but he will be a holy priest.' He certainly lived up to the description of being a holy priest. He served six years in the Parish of Wisconsin before leaving in 1956 to carry out his promise of five years of missionary work in South America. Little did he realise that five years would become fifty-six years, most of them spent in South America.

When he arrived in Santa Cruz, Bolivia, the bishop gave Fr Joe a machete to clear space in the jungle for a church. Father Joe was never one to shirk his responsibilities. He travelled to Brazil for cement and, when a bridge collapsed, he helped carry the cement bags to Santa Cruz. He persuaded the locals to help him carve out space in the jungle to build a church and a local school. During the construction of the church, he slept in a barn with livestock and a straw bed. During the early part of the construction, the church walls fell three times. Father Joe considered this providential, as Christ fell three times carrying his cross. When the church was finished, he named it the Holy Cross. The people were impoverished and the arrival of Fr Joseph was a Godsend to them. So great was the love they developed for him, that they travelled from all over to be near the priest and close to the church. From the depths of the jungle grew today's vibrant city of Santa Cruz de la Sierra, home to over one million people, with Santa Cruz Parish found just one block from the city centre. The parish now boasts over fifty thousand parishioners, with two thousand students annually receiving an education in the school that was also built by Fr Joe.

After his initial years in Bolivia, Fr Joe was recalled to serve in the parish in Wisconsin. However, he didn't remain long in his home parish. South America called to him once again when, in 1970, an earthquake struck Peru. Father Joe asked for permission to return as a missionary priest to help the Peruvian people recover from what was the worst natural disaster Peru had ever seen. Father Joe would spend the rest of his ministry faithfully serving some of the world's most impoverished people. It is said by those who knew him that his time in Peru was one of the most productive phases of his priesthood. Applying the skills he learned in Bolivia, Fr Joe soon set about the task of rebuilding and providing dwellings for the people of the shanty towns.

Father Joe once told the story of seeing piles of newspapers lying on street corners. When he looked closer, he realised that the papers were the sleeping quarters of homeless children. He asked himself how he could go home and enjoy a good night's sleep knowing that these children had no home, no proper bed and, worse still, no parents to care for them. He knew he had to do something. As a young boy, Fr Joe recalled seeing the movie *Boys Town*, based on the life of a man he admired greatly, Fr Edward Flanagan. The movie inspired him to emulate Fr Flanagan in his love for poor and orphaned children. Peru now provided the perfect backdrop for Fr Joe to create his own place for 'happy children'. As he always did when he needed to do the impossible, he relied on divine providence. Father Joe always said he was just a pencil in God's hands and anything he accomplished was through the grace of God. With this belief firmly in place, his quest for donations took him to Poland with the hope of having an audience with another Polish priest, Pope John Paul II.

In 1979, an estimated three million people, including Fr Joe, saw Pope John Paul in his native country. He desperately sought a meeting with the popular pope in the hope of raising awareness of the poverty in Peru. He had a friend in the pope's party who got Fr Joe close to the pope. They met – one Polish priest to another – and Fr Joe asked the pope to bless a loaf of bread, which is a Polish tradition. He invited Pope John Paul II to visit El Salvador and, in 1985, the pope obliged. He was happy for Fr Joe to introduce him to the massive crowd. Witnessing the extreme poverty for himself, Pope John Paul II gave the Cardinal of Lima a fifty-thousand-dollar donation for the poor. The cardinal knew the best man to give the money to, and Fr Joe received the donation necessary to build his orphanage. He named the orphanage Casa Hogar Juan Pablo II (The House Home of Pope John Paul II).

Father Joe's efforts in Peru resulted in him carving from the wilderness the Christ the Saviour Parish church in Lima, along with eight smaller chapels – one named St Joseph – throughout Villa El Salvador. Father Joe was pastor to one hundred thousand parishioners. Today, Christ the Saviour Parish serves some sixty-five thousand parishioners, provides a kindergarten for over one hundred children, and two food kitchens prepare some six hundred lunches every week for the poor. Father Joe once encountered a boy playing ball and he asked him why he was not at home having lunch. The boy's reply was that it was not his turn to eat that day. This interaction lead to the establishment of food kitchens throughout Villa El Salvador that are still in operation today. Following the lead of their founder, Fr Joe, the volunteer staff rely on God's providence to provide food for the hungry.

Perhaps one of his greatest achievements in South America was his orphanage, Casa Hogar. Here the children not only receive shelter from the storm, even more importantly, they receive the hope of a bright, positive future. Father Joe believed that if you are to transform society then you must teach children what it is to be part of a family. The family unit in Casa Hogar comes in the form of married couples who look after eight children a piece – boys in one family and girls in another. The children stay here until they reach seventeen, or they can leave sooner if their family background improves. The children are assigned chores and a sense of responsibility and self-worth, which helps them mature. They are tutored in Casa Hogar, as well as attending school, which gives them the possibility of qualifying for university. They are also instructed in their faith.

Not one to rest on his laurels, at eighty-one years of age, Fr Joe founded St Joseph's Retirement Home in a remote area in Peru. The home is run by religious Sisters. In 2006, Fr Joe celebrated Palm Sunday Mass. Two days later, he died of pneumonia. Such was the love the people had for their priest, mentor and father-figure to many, that his wake lasted for a week. Father Joe's selfless contribution to the poorest of the poor still remains intact. The churches, schools and orphanage he founded still flourish. In 2016, Pope Francis visited Holy Cross Parish, Santa Cruz, Bolivia, following in the footsteps of Fr Joe. The humble Polish priest who once said 'The greatest joy of being a Christian is to know you can serve others' has not been forgotten.

In 2013, Fr Joe's home parish of St Joseph, Wisconsin, began the cause for his canonisation on 19 March – the feast of St Joseph. If successful, Fr Joseph Walijewski will become a Saint of the Church he served so faithfully his entire priestly life.

Father Emil Kapaun

The Soldiers' Chaplin

In 1953, following the end of the Korean War, a group of American soldiers emerged from Pyoktong POW camp. The men carried a wooden crucifix that bore a crown of thorns constructed from radio wire. The soldier who made the crucifix was not, in fact, Catholic, but Jewish. What prompted this POW to construct the cross was his great love for Fr Emil Kapaun, the army chaplain from Kansas who laid down his life for his men, regardless of their religious beliefs. Father Kapaun not only received the Medal of Honour some sixty years after his death in 1951, but, in 1993, was declared Servant of God. The Diocese of Wichita, Kansas, in conjunction with the Vatican, has begun formal proceedings that could see Fr Kapaun canonised.

What led to this humble army chaplain who served in World War II and the Korean War being recognised for bravery on the field of battle and recommended for sainthood? Much of his recognition begins with the soldiers he served with in Korea in 1950 and whose lives he changed forever. 'How could you ever forget a man who saved your life?' Sergeant Herbert Miller asked. Miller recounted how Fr Kapaun stepped between him and the soldier about to shoot him as he lay wounded in a ditch. He recalled Fr Kapaun pushing the soldier to the side, bending down and lifting him from the ditch. Why that Korean soldier did not shoot Fr Kapaun remained a mystery to Miller. Even under heavy fire, Fr Kapaun carried wounded men to a dugout where others, including a Chinese officer, were taking shelter. When they were eventually overrun, Fr Kapaun refused to escape, opting to stay with the men. He successfully negotiated with the Chinese officer to have the men taken prisoner rather than be executed by the advancing Chinese.

As they were being marched some thirty miles to Pyoktong prison camp, Fr Kapaun carried Sergeant Miller. He knew if he left the wounded soldier, he would be shot. The long march from Unsan to Pyoktong became known as the Death March. It stuck in the mind of Lieutenant Mike Dowe who, although having heard of the padre, first encountered him on this march. Father Kapaun kept their morale high, Dowe recalled, and, through example, motivated the soldiers to help carry the wounded. The lieutenant spoke of the incredible bravery of Fr Kapaun in the face of unbelievable odds. It was told that wherever the wounded lay, the chaplain made it his business to be by their side. He ignored heavy gunfire to bring comfort and relief to the injured and dying and to see to their spiritual needs. Mike Dowe, like many others, was at a loss to understand how Fr Kapaun seemed to run rings around the Communist soldiers and not get shot himself. It must have been the intervention of God that saved the padre, Dowe concluded.

Remembering Fr Kapaun during his time in the POW camp, Dowe commented, 'This guy did one thing after another for a good six months before they finally killed him. He saved close to a thousand lives.' Lieutenant Dowe worked tirelessly for decades to ensure that Fr Kapaun got the military recognition he deserved for his bravery. Countless soldiers thanked him for making the harshest conditions in the camp survivable. They spoke of enduring a bitter winter in summer clothes with Fr Kapaun scrounging around for food and caring for the wounded. He never regarded his own needs, Dowe said, just those of others. Even when the guards threatened to shoot him, he carried on regardless, doing what he could for the men. The guards could never break him; he was more than a match for them, the soldiers recalled. When the Chinese took him, as they did others, to torture and 'educate', he resisted their brainwashing. They were plain afraid of him, Dowe recalled. They didn't know how to treat someone as fearless as this priest; that's why they wanted him dead. They feared him more than he feared them.

Father Kapaun continually prayed with the men. He stimulated their will to live when many were ready to give up. Lieutenant Dowe recalled Fr Kapaun praying to St Dismas, the 'Good Thief', to grant him success during his foraging missions. Then he would sneak out to get extra corn and other food for the men. Dowe remembered him coming back with wood for the fire and making pans out of roofing tin to boil water. 'Hot coffee,' Fr Kapaun would quip. Dowe said it's what helped sustain them: 'he got us through days and nights of deprivation.' Dowe spoke of two other POW camps in the same valley where the men died at an alarming rate. However, the rate of those who died in Fr Kapaun's camp was one-tenth of the other two. During his seven months as a POW, Fr Kapaun spent this time in heroic service to his fellow prisoners. He would go from hut to hut praying the rosary. He ignored his own ill health to attend to the men until a blood clot in his leg prevented him from making his daily rounds. Lieutenant Dowe recalled being with the padre, who was suffering from pneumonia, when the Chinese guards removed him to the camp's 'hospital' where he was denied medical assistance. Dowe described the so-called hospital as a bug- and maggot-infested room named the 'death house' because no one ever came out of it alive. Even though the padre's fever had broken, the guards would not let him leave the hospital as they feared he may recover. Father Kapaun spoke to the men and told them not to put up any resistance as he feared they would be shot. He said to Mike Dowe, 'Don't cry, Mike. I'm going to where I always wanted to go. When I get there, I'll say a prayer for all of you.' Father Kapaun died in May 1951. His legacy refused to die, however, and the good padre posthumously received the Distinguished Service Cross in 1951.

Many stories have been told and books written about Fr Kapaun. The journalist Roy Wenzl, who co-wrote the book, *The Miracle of Father Kapaun*, was initially sceptical until he interviewed former POWs all over the country. Listening to the men's stories helped change his mind. Wenzl believed that the priest's resourcefulness in making pots to boil water saved many from dysentery.

Andrea Ambrosi, a Vatican lawyer, has investigated two alleged miracles attributed to Fr Kapaun's intercession. In 2006, a twelve-year-old girl named Avery Gerleman was dying from major organ failure. Much to the astonishment of her doctors, Avery recovered after her parents prayed to Fr Kapaun. In 2008, Chase Kear, a college athlete, survived a pole-vaulting accident. His skull was fractured from ear to ear, causing bleeding on his brain. Doctors said he would either die in surgery or from a post-surgery infection. However, family and friends prayed to Fr Kapaun. Kear survived the surgery and left the hospital weeks after the incident. Doctors said both recoveries were medically inexplicable. Ambrosi said the intensity of the priest's devotees is incredible. Several Catholic parishes pray for Fr Kapaun's intercession when loved ones become ill.

Father John Hotze, working for Fr Kapaun's canonisation, commented that he exemplified Christian love, even the love of enemies, blessing his captors as they took him to the 'death house' and asking forgiveness for them. Father Hotze said that the diocese has finished collecting information that will hopefully lead to Fr Kapaun's canonisation. In addition, countless people claim to have received physical and spiritual healing and conversions to the faith through Fr Kapaun's intercession.

The soldiers who walked out of the death camps of North Korea were Fr Kapaun's legacy. Their testimony and those of contemporary accounts could set Fr Emile Kapaun on the road to sainthood and give America another saint.

Belfast's Christian Brothers

To Do and To Teach

When first introduced in 1831, Ireland's national educational system was aimed at providing secular education to all children. Religious instruction, if any, was for after-school hours. This met with fierce resistance from the major Churches, who considered education to be an extension of pastoral care and, as such, it should not be separated from religious instruction. The move was viewed by the Churches as an intrusion of the State into their sphere of influence.

Such was the opposition to the secular proposals that the commissioners were eventually forced to renege and allow schools to become denominational. Some thirty years later, in 1866, the Bishop of Down and Connor,

Dr Dorrian, succeeded in encouraging the Christian Brothers to come to Belfast and open their first school – St Mary's in Divis Street.

Four Brothers – Caton, Neaton, Maguire and Ennis – arrived in November of that year to form the first community of Brothers in Belfast. Their aim was to educate the children of the working class, many of whom came from Belfast's overcrowded and impoverished areas.

Their reputation as educators was so great that the school had to turn many boys away as it was not large enough to accommodate them all. Saint Mary's proved to be such a success that a second school was deemed necessary and, by 1867, four more Brothers arrived in Belfast to take charge of St Patrick's in Donegall Street, with an intake of four hundred and fifty pupils.

The Brothers opened their third school, St Malachy's in Oxford Street in 1874. The cost of construction, £2,400, was met by a charitable donor called Mrs McGill who wanted the school located closer to the quays to serve the children of sailors and dock labourers. Intermediate exams were first held in 1879 and fourteen boys successfully passed their examinations. The McGill family were so impressed that a further £50 donation was made. The school went on to further distinguish itself with its pupils' examination results.

In 1900, the Belfast Corporation introduced Technical Education. Relying on the success of the previous schools, the Brother Superior, T.P. Ryan, was granted a share of the funds available to teach Technical Education. The money was channelled into Hardinge Street Trade School. When the school opened in 1903, it boasted physics and chemistry laboratories and a lecture room. Here the boys could study a range of subjects from Science, Maths and Modern Languages to Woodwork. With the true zeal of their founder, Blessed Edmund Rice, the Brothers' impact on education resulted in the school achieving first place throughout Ireland in Chemistry, two second places in Maths and Science, third place in English, and two Royal College of Science scholarships, among other accolades.

The Christian Brothers gave boys from poor families an education their parents could never have afforded. It enabled many of them to take their place among the professional classes of Belfast and beyond.

The success of Hardinge Street Trade School saw educational demand outstrip supply. To meet the insatiable demand from the Catholic populace, in 1929 the Brothers opened yet another secondary school, St Mary's Grammar School in Barrack Street, Belfast. Victims of their own success, St Mary's struggled with accommodation problems. The demand for places was compounded with the introduction of the Northern Ireland 1947 Education Act. The Act made education compulsory for all children up to the age of fifteen. Primary education ended at eleven and demand for secondary level education increased.

Eager to keep up with demands, the Brothers eventually opened St Mary's CBS in 1968 on the Glen Road, Belfast, with an intake of 1,320 pupils. Barrack Street continued to serve the city centre and accommodated pupils from the outer city. It eventually closed its doors in 1998, after some seventy years of serving and educating many Belfast children. However, the closure of one school saw the opening of many more. From the sixties on, the Brothers opened nearly a dozen primary and secondary schools throughout Belfast to accommodate the growing number of male pupils.

The Christian Brothers' contribution to the educational needs of many impoverished Catholic children in Belfast, and their willingness to answer the educational call, has not been forgotten. In November 2016, a Mass commemorating their arrival in Belfast one hundred and fifty years previously was celebrated in St Mary's Church, Chapel Lane. Bishop Noel Trainor presided at the Mass and Bishop Patrick Walsh was the main celebrant. Father Tim Bartlett gave the homily. All three are former pupils of the Christian Brothers. Bishop Walsh was named the outstanding student of his year when he obtained a first in the Senior Leaving Certificate. He went on to win two exhibitions in Literature and Science. His celebration of the Mass was followed by a reception and exhibition in the Westcourt Centre, Barrack Street. The exhibition was attended by many former pupils, now in their fifties, sixties and seventies, who went on to become doctors, lawyers, teachers and engineers, among many other things. Each was there to remember with fondness their school days and the first-class education they received from the Christian Brothers.

Father Patrick Peyton

The Rosary Priest

As a boy in Co. Mayo, Patrick found his calling to the priesthood. The sixth of nine children, he grew up on a farm where hard work and nightly family rosaries helped form his character and that of his siblings. Due to lack of education and funds for the seminary, Patrick was initially turned down for the priesthood. Disheartened, he considered making his millions in America selling real estate. Before their father gave permission to Patrick and his older brother, Thomas, to leave for America, he made them promise, on their knees in front of the picture of the Sacred Heart, to follow their own counsel and no one else's. He told them their first responsibility was to save their souls and to always remain faithful to God, no matter where they were.

In May 1928, at nineteen years of age, Patrick and Thomas sailed to America. They weren't the first of their family to emigrate – three of their sisters were already settled in America by the time they landed in New York. They headed for the Electric City, Scranton, Pennsylvania, where Thomas got work in a coal mine. Patrick was not fit enough to work down the mines so he secured a job as a caretaker in St Peter's Cathedral. The religious atmosphere of the cathedral, along with a mission given by the Holy Cross Priests in 1929, resurrected a desire within the brothers to enter religious life. Patrick later remembered that the calling became so strong that he could not dismiss it from his mind. For him, there was nothing better than following Christ. In the same year, both brothers entered Notre Dame Holy Cross Seminary, Indiana. In 1932, aged twenty-three, Patrick graduated and began his novitiate at Holy Cross Seminary.

At the end of the brothers' priestly training, Patrick favoured missionary work. However, he suffered a severe health setback. In 1938, he was diagnosed with advanced tuberculosis. The doctors could offer him little hope of recovery. While in hospital he was visited by his mentor, Holy Cross Father Cornelius Hagerty. Father Hagerty reminded Patrick of his strong faith: 'You have faith, Pat. You're just not using it. You brought it with you from

Ireland. Your mother gave it to you, just as her mother had given it to her.' Father Hagerty can perhaps be accredited as the priest who set Fr Peyton on his path as a rosary crusader. He reminded Patrick that the prayers of the rosary never go unheard. 'The Blessed Mother never failed anyone who had recourse to her with faith and perseverance,' he reminded Patrick. With renewed vigour, Patrick Peyton prayed the rosary for a cure. His prayers were answered: on 31 October 1939, he was cured of tuberculosis.

One of his greatest gifts arrived in 1941, one year after his mother's death, when he was ordained to the priesthood alongside his brother, Thomas. Father Patrick said, 'That day I gave my heart and soul in love to Mary.' The brothers sent a photo of their ordination back home. Their father, gravely ill at the time, wrote his last letter to them. He spoke of his joy at living to see them both received into the priesthood. He encouraged them to remain faithful to their calling.

Father Patrick's missionary quest was how to spread devotion to our Blessed Mother through the rosary. He pondered how to reach millions of families in their homes. Coming from a close-knit family himself, he realised the value of family unity. The way to promote this, he knew, was to encourage family rosaries. The saying most associated with Fr Peyton's name was born:

'The family that prays together, stays together.' He elicited the help of Brothers, Sisters and students from the Vincentian Institute to assist him in writing letters to bishops asking for their help. He realised that the way to reach countless households was through the mass media. Among those he approached for help was the well-known and established Monsignor Fulton Sheen, who went on to become archbishop in 1969. Father Sheen invited his listeners to write to his radio show requesting free rosary beads and a rosary book, all to be provided by Fr Peyton. The archbishop advised Fr Peyton to expect some ten thousand requests. Such was the interest that by the end of the second week, the station was flooded with over fifty-six thousand people requesting rosary beads. Catholics and non-Catholics were eager to pray to the Blessed Mother for assistance in their everyday lives.

Encouraged by the response, Fr Peyton headed for New York to continue his missionary work. He was granted permission to broadcast over the largest radio network in America at the time, the Mutual Broadcasting Company. However, it came with a proviso: he had to provide a Hollywood personality to share the platform with him. He rang Bing Crosby, who gladly agreed to do the show. The show aired on 13 May 1945. The date was propitious. Not only was it the feast of Our Lady of Fatima, it was also

Mothers' Day and a day of thanksgiving for the ending of hostilities in Europe. The rosary crusader reached families nationwide, including President Harry Truman, who lent his considerable weight to the proceedings. The rosary prayers encouraged families to pray for peace. The presence of Mr and Mrs Sullivan was particularly poignant. Their five sons died when their boat, the *Juneau*, was torpedoed in 1942. The show was extremely successful and the public wanted more.

Father Peyton's next religious journey took him to California, where he made contact with fellow priests in the Archdiocese of Los Angeles. At Good Shepherd Parish in Beverley Hills, Fr Peyton made the acquaintance of many of Hollywood's leading stars, including Loretta Young, who helped him get established in Hollywood.

A host of top Hollywood names, including Maureen O'Hara, Grace Kelly, James Cagney and Bing Crosby, agreed to help Fr Peyton in his mission to spread rosary devotion throughout the world. They gave willingly of their time to help Fr Peyton. However, it was not all plain sailing. While interested in his proposals, Mutual Broadcasting laid down strict conditions. They informed Fr Peyton that he had to finance the show and no mention of religion was to be made. The rosary could only be promoted through commercials on the show.

Undeterred, Fr Peyton founded a family, faith-based production company called Family Theater Productions. Many star-studded names, from Jack Benny to Kirk Douglas to Maureen O'Hara continued to entertain listeners and the show ran for some twenty-two years. The show's motto 'The family that prays together, stays together' became famous. By 1952, they were broadcasting nationwide to 460 stations and worldwide on the armed forces radio. Father Peyton launched a nationwide billboard campaign encouraging family prayer, which was his recommended staple diet for wholesome family life.

In 1954, Fr Peyton brought his worldwide rosary crusade to Ireland. Parish after parish turned out in their thousands to welcome the Rosary Priest. In Belfast alone, over one hundred thousand people took part in the rosary crusade. In the Diocese of Down and Connor, almost 163,000 people – ninety-eight per cent of the Catholic population – signed the Rosary Pledge, promising to recite the daily rosary.

Father Peyton has been described as a dynamic advocate for family prayer, a trailblazer, and – like Archbishop Fulton Sheen before him – a television evangelist. Father Peyton died in California 1992 and is buried in Massachusetts. Since his death there have been many reports of physical healing and spiritual favours received. Many lapsed Catholics have attributed their return to the Church to the intercession of Fr Peyton.

In 2001, at the request of the Congregation of Holy Cross, Massachusetts, the Vatican officially opened the cause of canonisation. At that time, Fr Peyton was given the title Servant of God.

In 1998, The Father Peyton CSC Memorial Centre was officially opened in his birthplace of Attymass Parish, Co. Mayo. The centre hopes to continue the mission of Fr Peyton by promoting family rosaries. This is a fitting legacy to a priest credited with doing more to inspire devotion to Our Lady and the rosary than anyone in history.

Archbishop Fulton J. Sheen

Life is Worth Living

While serving at Mass in Peoria, Illinois, an eight-year-old altar boy dropped the wine cruet on the floor. After Mass, Bishop Spalding spoke to the frightened altar boy. He didn't reprimand him for the spill but, instead, informed the boy that one day he would study at Louvain College in Belgium and would go on to become a bishop. These were prophetic words. Not only did the young boy go on to study at Louvain, he went on to host his own television show. He would become a household name for millions of Americans who eagerly tuned in to watch Archbishop Fulton J. Sheen present his weekly show, *Life is Worth Living.*

In 1919, the young Peter John Sheen progressed to the priesthood at the age of twenty-four. Continuing his studies in the Catholic University of America, Fr Sheen left in 1921 to read Philosophy at Louvain College. The five years he spent in advanced studies marked him out at the prestigious university. He was the first American to be invited back to the college to participate in post-doctorate studies. In his autobiography, *Treasure in Clay*, he spoke of the post-doctorate. 'If you passed this exam for professorship with satisfaction,' he said, 'only water could be served at the dinner; if with distinction, beer, if with great distinction, wine; and with the very highest distinction, champagne. The champagne tasted so good that night!'

The eldest of four boys from El Paso, Illinois, Peter John Sheen and his brothers were handed on the faith from his parents. From an Irish background, the farming family prayed the daily rosary with their children. When Peter John was baptised, his mother placed him on Our Lady's altar and consecrated her young son to the Blessed Virgin. It was a Marian devotion Archbishop Sheen carried with him his entire life. The Sheen family were noted for their intelligence and hard work. Fulton, who took his name from his mother's side, was an avid reader. It was said he could read a book in an hour and was known to work nineteen-hour days. His deep, penetrating eyes and rousing rhetoric captivated audiences.

His oratory skills were fine-tuned during his twenty-three-year tenure at the Catholic University of America in Washington DC. He entered the college in 1927 and was quickly recognised as a brilliant educator, scholar and evangelist. Lecturing in Theology, Religious Studies and Philosophy, students and visitors alike crowded into the lecture halls to hear one of the greatest orators of the twentieth century. He gave talks on a wide range of subjects to students and radio listeners. Never turning down a chance to speak, he accepted an invite to preach in St Patrick's Cathedral, New York. Such was his popularity that thousands of people turned out to hear him. The police had to close off Fifth Avenue to accommodate the crowds who stood outside to listen.

His teaching was so enlightening that in one year alone he received up to one hundred letters a day, from people of all walks of life. Bishops, priests, students, converts and non-Catholics wrote to him requesting further instruction on wide-ranging topics. In 1937, he wrote to University Rector Monsignor Joseph Corrigan, informing him that between the correspondences and lectures, he was exhausted. However, he was not complaining of work overload, he just needed God's help to continue with his apostolate. Fulton J. Sheen's reputation was so great that in 1934, at the age of thirty-nine, he came to the attention of Pope Pius XI who made him a Monsignor.

Among the countless thank-you notes he received, one came from Robert Sproul, President of the University of California. Sproul thanked Monsignor Sheen for the two talks he gave in 1938 to his body of students on the topic 'Liberty, Equality and Fraternity'. President Sproul said of Fulton Sheen, 'He literally held the group spellbound by the clarity of his thinking and the artistry of his speaking. His address was generally considered to be the best of its kind we have heard at the university in many years.'

By 1940, Fulton Sheen found himself confined to bed in a New York hospital suffering from exhaustion. He was ordered by his doctor to rest or suffer a complete physical and mental breakdown. Never one to shirk his responsibilities, however, Fr Sheen was soon back on his feet, travelling the country, giving lectures, and leading missions and retreats.

Politically astute and outspoken, Monsignor Sheen warned of the dangers of Communism and America's naivety in believing they had an ally in Moscow against German fascism. Monsignor Sheen was hypercritical of both regimes. He denounced Russia as the Red Peril and predicted that Germany would collapse internally with mass suicides, including that of Hitler. With far-sighted and prophetic vision, Fulton Sheen predicted that Germany and Russia would unite as they both shared totalitarian views. His denouncements were so strong that he came to the attention of the FBI who opened a file on him and closely monitored his political comments.

In 1948, alongside Cardinal Spellman of New York, Monsignor Sheen travelled the world giving talks. In 1950, the cardinal made Fulton Sheen Head of the Society for the Propagation of Faith. Resigning as a teacher of Philosophy from the Catholic University to take up his new role, Monsignor Sheen spoke fondly of his time there: 'After twenty-three years of happy association, I take leave of the Catholic University academically, but not spiritually.' An even busier time was ahead when he was consecrated a bishop in 1951 and served as Auxiliary Bishop of the Archdiocese of New York until 1965.

As one of the best-known Catholic evangelists of his time, his next sojourn launched him even further into the world of celebrity. His weekly television series, *Life is Worth Living,* broadcast live during the 1950s, brought in an audience of thirty million viewers each week. He worked without cue cards or notes, yet always managed to finish each show on time. His competitors – Milton Berle, a popular comedian, and Frank Sinatra – took second place to him. Fulton Sheen won an Emmy Award in 1952 for Most Outstanding Television Personality. Accepting the award, Sheen, with typical humour, said he wanted to thank his writers Matthew, Mark, Luke and John. Appearing on the American panel show *What's My Line?* in 1956, he asked that the money he received be sent to dozens of leper colonies. He featured on the cover of *Time* magazine and was considered one of the most influential Catholics of the twentieth century.

Through television, radio and personal appearances, Fulton Sheen raised millions of dollars for his favourite charitable cause – the poor. He helped parishes at home and in Africa, and he found it impossible to pass a beggar on the street. When out walking with his niece Joan, she observed the number of people who would stop him and ask for a few dollars, which they always got. She asked her uncle, 'How do you know they are not putting you on?' He replied, 'I can't take the chance'. Joan also spoke of her uncle's neat and tidy appearance. He informed her, 'I'm an ambassador of Christ'.

'People always gave him things,' Joan once told an interviewer. He received a new Cadillac every two years from a grateful dealer in Washington DC. The dealer had informed her uncle that he was having serious trouble with his employees. The bishop advised him to profit share with them. The advice worked and the man's business improved.

Archbishop Sheen was generous to a fault. It was his generosity and love of helping the poor that saw him cross swords with the powerful Cardinal Francis Joseph Spellman. Sheen was successfully fundraising for the missions at a time when the cardinal's collections were showing a financial shortfall. Sheen contributed a vast amount of his own money to charity. When the cardinal wanted Sheen to pay money to the archdiocese, Sheen refused. Spellman was outraged that a subordinate would defy him and took the matter to Rome. Pope Pius XII sided with Archbishop Sheen. Not to be outdone, Spellman informed Sheen, 'I will get even with you. It may take six months or ten years.'

True to his word, Cardinal Spellman religiously blackballed Fulton Sheen. His appearances on *Life is Worth Living* ended. Sheen's annual Good Friday sermons in St Patrick's Cathedral were cancelled. Priests within the Diocese of New York were informed not to invite Archbishop Sheen to their parishes, to officiate at Mass or to preach. In 1966, Cardinal Spellman sent Fulton to the Diocese of Rochester in upstate New York, which was considered to be 'ecclesiastical Siberia'. He terminated Sheen's leadership of the Society for the

Propagation of the Faith, a position Sheen had held for sixteen years.

Archbishop Sheen rarely spoke of the tussle with Cardinal Spellman. He even spoke favourably of him in his autobiography. Cardinal Spellman died in 1967, twelve years before Fulton Sheen.

Archbishop Sheen wrote some seventy books, countless articles and brought numerous converts into the faith, including the motor industrialist Henry Ford II. He continues to inspire television audiences with reruns of his show *Life is Worth Living*. In 2002, the cause for his canonisation was opened. For the declared Venerable Servant of God, Fulton J. Sheen, life was very much worth living.

Father Solanus Casey

The Priest Who Answered the Doorbell

Ireland's loss was America's gain when emigrants Bernard Casey and Ellen Murphy separately left the Emerald Isle following Ireland's Great Hunger of 1845. In 1857, at the age of seventeen, Bernard James Casey and a younger sister left their homeland of Castleblayney, Co. Monaghan to make the perilous sea crossing. His widowed mother's parting words to her son were, 'Barney, boy, keep the faith.' Sailing from Liverpool, the brother and sister arrived in Boston where they were reunited with relatives. Bernard found skilful employment as a shoemaker. Unbeknownst to the young man, his future wife, who arrived in America five years earlier, was waiting to make his acquaintance.

Ellen Murphy hailed from Camlough in the orchard county of Armagh. She had travelled with her family to Boston in 1852, when she was eight years old. Similar in many ways to Bernard Casey, the newly arrived immigrants stayed with relatives who were already settled in the New World. As a young woman, Ellen found work in a textile mill near Portland, Maine. It would be some eight years before the pair would encounter each other at a Fourth of July picnic in Biddeford, Maine. One account relates that when Ellen and Bernard met, it was love at first sight. Ellen was sixteen years of age at the time, four years younger than Bernard, and her mother insisted on a waiting period of three years before her daughter would have parental consent to marry Bernard.

During that three-year separation, the young couple lost contact with each other. Determined to find his sweetheart, Bernard elicited the help of his parish priest. His endeavours proved successful and the young couple were eventually married in St James Church in Salem, Massachusetts, in 1863. Three years later, following the cessation of the American Civil War, Bernard and Ellen upped stakes and secured eighty acres of government land in Prescott, Wisconsin, where Bernard, their sixth child, was born in 1870. Staying within the farming community, the young family moved again to a larger farm.

Life was not always idyllic for the Caseys and their sixteen children, three of whom would become priests. During a diphtheria outbreak, Ellen and Bernard lost two of their daughters. Barney also contracted the disease, leaving his voice slightly impaired and wispy. Crop failure and wildfires were also part of life for many farm residents. When fires threatened their farm, the Casey family prayed the rosary, asking that their holdings be spared. It instilled in the young Barney a firm, unshakable belief in the power of prayer, a lesson that sustained him throughout his long religious life. Father Solanus often recalled his father calling out to them, 'Prayer, boys, prayer!' He recalled that prayer life for the family began every day in their home with family rosary, and night prayers began promptly at 7 p.m. every evening.

Working outside the farm, Barney had a series of jobs from logger to streetcar operator to prison guard. His family were hard-working and diligent. There were so many of them that they even had their own baseball team. The siblings enjoyed the many outdoor activities that their environment offered. Their youthful energies found an outlet in skiing, hunting, skating, fishing and swimming. The boys enjoyed the rough and tumble of boxing, a sport Barney shunned as the idea of inflicting pain on another didn't appeal to him. He recalled that he used to play his fiddle at the local barn dances. Their family entertainment consisted of a favourite Irish pastime – storytelling. They also gathered around for a singsong of Irish and American folk songs, no doubt with Barney on his fiddle.

Like most young men, Barney was in favour of finding a wife. However, the young girl he was interested in was sent off to boarding school. That door in his life closed, but an even greater one was about to open. During his working life, he witnessed the fatal stabbing of a young woman at the hands of a drunken sailor. His biographer wrote, 'The scene remained with him. To him, the brutal stabbing and the sailor's hysterical cursing symbolised the world's sin and hate and man-made misery.'[5] It was a crime that awoke a desire within the heart and soul of the gentle Barney for the religious life.

In his twenty-first year, Barney set off on his path to the priesthood and, unbeknownst to him at that time, that path would eventually lead him towards sainthood. The young postulant's entry into holy orders was not without difficulty, however. Saint Francis Seminary in Milwaukee, Wisconsin, taught classes through the medium of German and Latin. These were two languages Barney found impossible to grasp. At the suggestion of his superiors, he looked for outside help. He asked his mother and sister Ellen to join him in praying a nine-day novena. On the last day of the novena, Barney attended Mass and, after Communion, he heard the voice of the Blessed Mother telling him to go to Detroit, where the Capuchin Friars had their monastery.

Barney entered the Capuchin Order in 1896 at the age of twenty-six, taking the name Solanus after the patron saint St Francis Solanus, the Spanish missionary to Peru. Never noted for his academic prowess, Solanus was ordained to the priesthood eight years later as a 'simplex priest', which was a priest who did not have the ability to hear confessions or preach doctrinal sermons. The newly ordained Solanus never displayed any kind of resentment; he gratefully accepted his humble role in the service of Christ, closely adhering to his vows of poverty, chastity and obedience.

Father Solanus's roles in service to the Church – whether in New York or Detroit – ranged from sacristan to doorkeeper to director of altar boys. His role within the Capuchin Order was described as humble. Whether he was tasked with doing odd jobs or carrying messages to his fellow priests, he did it all willingly and without complaint.

In the service of Christ, Fr Solanus exuded such inner grace and sanctity that those whose path he crossed were drawn back to him for spiritual help and guidance. The humble friar's reputation as a healer quickly spread, and soon people were seeking him out, requesting prayers of healing for themselves and their family members. Many waited in line for hours to see the simplex priest with the charism for healing and, many believed, prophecy.

At the behest of his superior, Solanus kept a record of healings and miraculous cures attributed to him, filling up several notebooks. He had a deep love for the poor and destitute. During America's Great Depression of 1929, Solanus helped inspire the Capuchins of Detroit to establish a soup kitchen that is still in existence to this day. As the Depression worsened, the Capuchin soup kitchen, which at times fed more than one thousand people a day, found itself out of bread. With unshakable faith in the power of prayer, Fr Solanus rose, blessed the soup kitchen aloud and urged his brothers to be confident in God. Within moments, an entire truckload of donated bread arrived at the kitchen door.

Stories abound of miraculous cures attributed to the humble priest. His notebook entries contain cures ranging from pneumonia, alcoholism, tuberculosis, cancer and paralysis. He humbly brushed aside the spiritual healings and conversions to the Church that took place in his name. He contributed nothing to himself and everything to the collective prayers of the missionaries and, of course, his Blessed Lord, of whom he said, 'The good God is a loving God. He just wants to fill needs'. He always thanked God in advance when asking for a favour or cure. When asked by a fellow friar for an explanation, Solanus – with a twinkle in his eye – said that he liked to put God on the spot.

Another entry in his notebooks recorded a drunk man looking for Solanus at his monastery so he could kill him. The man was a Communist and his mother, a Catholic and friend of Solanus, implored the friar to pray for her son. To prevent Solanus from influencing his mother, the drunk man thought it best to kill the priest. Father Solanus invited him into the monastery and pacified him. Listening to the humble servant of God, the man rebuked his Communist beliefs and returned to the Church.

Father Solanus spent every day deep in prayer before the Blessed Sacrament. His prayers were always for others. On many occasions his fellow friars found him asleep on the chapel floor after a night of intensive prayer. While respecting those from other faiths, the humble friar – a true evangelist – encouraged conversions from those who came to see him.

In the tradition of their founder, St Francis, Solanus had a way with animals – even the stinging variety. The friars kept beehives. One particular friar had a fear of being stung by the bees. Once, when sent into the apple orchard, he quickly picked the apples and when he was about to leave, he noticed Solanus sitting in the orchard playing his fiddle with numerous bees sitting on the fiddle. Startled, the friar shouted to Solanus to be careful as the bees could sting him. Solanus stopped playing and the bees turned their attention to the startled friar who decided to flee. The bees attacked, stinging the unfortunate priest on his face, neck and hands. With no protective clothing, Solanus reached into the hive and removed a queen bee, placing her in an adjoining field. The bees broke off the attack and followed the queen, leaving the friar with serious stings. Solanus returned to the injured friar, placed his hands on him and eased the stinging pain. Later, when the doctor arrived at the monastery, he could not understand how the friar was still alive as the countless stings were enough to have killed him.

Father Solanus Casey said, 'I have two loves: the sick and the poor'. Those who knew him either personally or indirectly returned that love when over twenty thousand mourners attended his funeral in Detroit in 1957. The priest died at the age of eighty-six from erysipelas, a skin disease. During his final illness he said, 'I'm offering my sufferings that all might be one. If only I could see the conversion of the whole world'. Just before he passed away, he sat up in bed and proclaimed, 'I give my soul to Jesus Christ'. The humble servant of God died on the same day and hour on which he said his first ever Mass.

Death took Fr Solanus Casey's body but not his legacy. It lives on, growing stronger and spreading around the world. The number of devotees visiting his grave was so great that Church authorities exhumed his body in 1987. It was clothed in a new habit and reinterred in a metal casket in St Bonaventure Church, Detroit. The story didn't end there. In 1995, Fr Solanus was declared venerable. Twenty-two years later, Detroit city had the honour of hosting the Beatification Mass of Fr Solanus. Thousands flooded into Ford Field stadium to share in the honour of witnessing the humble friar's step towards sainthood. It is believed the crowds outnumbered those who turned out to greet Pope John Paul II in 1987, when he presided over a Mass in Pontiac, Michigan.

Like a spiritual celebrity, he still pulls in his fans. Sixty-four years after his death, the Solanus Casey Spiritual Centre receives two hundred and fifty thousand visitors every year. Reports of cures attributed to the humble friar still abound. The priest who answered the door to all callers has opened an even greater doorway to Heaven, for not only himself, but for his legion of followers.

When his father, Bernard Casey, left his Irish homeland, his mother's parting words were, 'Barney, boy. Keep the faith'. Bernard senior did keep the faith and, more importantly, he passed it on to his children. Without that Catholic faith, Fr Solanus Casey and his two brothers may never have entered the priesthood. Countless miracles of healings and repaired lives, attributed to Solanus, may never have come to pass. What better way to pay tribute to Detroit's saint in the making than to use his own words: 'God made me to know him. Oh what a blessed day. God bless you all.'

Saint Maximilian Kolbe

Greater Love Hath No Man

One of the first things to assail the eye is the chilling German motto *Arbeit macht frei* (Work sets you free). Written in large letters, it stands above the entrance of the most infamous of all the German concentration camps – Auschwitz. Originally a Polish Army barracks in southern Poland, Auschwitz was developed by the Nazis in 1940, a year after they invaded Poland. It was intended to be used as a jail to house political prisoners, but quickly grew into a means of mass extermination of Europe's Jewish population. In over four years, Auschwitz witnessed the deaths of over 1.1 million men, women and children, during one of the most horrific periods in human history. Almost one million of those who lost their lives in this terrifying camp were Jews. They were killed in many awful ways – in the gas chambers, through starvation or overwork, or by being the subject of barbaric medical experiments in the notorious medical wing.

One of the many who met an agonising death in Auschwitz was St Maximilian Kolbe. Known as the Saint of Auschwitz, the forty-seven-year-old Polish priest laid down his life for his fellow man. He willingly starved to death in the place of a man who was a complete stranger to him.

Rajmund Kolbe was born to German and Polish parents – Julius and Maria – in 1894 in Wola, Poland, which was then part of the Russian Empire. The second of five sons, the young Rajmund was once scolded by his mother for mischievous behaviour. Being sensitive to the reprimand, the boy asked in a prayerful way what would become of him, a Child of Faith? He later recalled receiving a vision of the Virgin Mary holding two crowns – one white and one red. The Mother of God asked which one he would accept – the white one meant he should persevere in purity and the red one was for martyrdom. Rajmund Kolbe chose both.

At the young age of thirteen, Rajmund and his older brother entered religious life, enrolling in the Franciscan seminary in Lwów, part of the Austrian-Hungarian empire. While attending Mass in the minor seminary, with his face to the ground, he promised the Blessed Virgin, whose image overlooked the altar, that he would fight for her. At that juncture in his life, he thought the fight would involve material weapons. He was soon to find out his battle would be of another kind.

In 1910, at the age of sixteen, Rajmund was admitted as an initiate, taking the religious name Maximilian. Four years later he took his final vows as a monk. Continuing with his studies, he went to Rome to study for his Doctorate in Philosophy at the Pontifical Gregorian University. By 1919 he gained a Doctorate of Theology from the University of St Bonaventure. One source quotes that Maximilian had a great interest in astrophysics and was enthused at the prospect of space flight. While studying in Rome he designed an aeroplane-type spacecraft, similar in design to the American space shuttle.

During his time as a student in Rome, he witnessed vehement demonstrations against Popes St Pius X and Benedict XV by the Freemasons. The anti-Catholic protests, declaring that Satan was going to reign, inspired the young monk to establish the Militia Immaculatae – the Army of Mary. Maximilian witnessed an army of masonic foot soldiers, intent on the destruction of the Catholic Church.

To counter this movement, the young religious was driven to start his own army of spiritual warriors, dedicated to Mary. The sole purpose of the organisation, which is worldwide today, was to actively seek the conversion of sinners and the enemies of the Catholic Church through the intercession of the Virgin Mary. Maximilian added the name Maria to his own to show his love for the Mother of God. The movement had its own printing press, magazine publications and books. The Catholic conservative tone of the articles often condemned Freemasonry, Communism, Zionism, Capitalism and Imperialism. It was as a result of his zeal for evangelisation that he incurred the wrath of his detractors, who attempted to accuse him of anti-Semitism.

In 1919, Maximilian returned to the newly independent Poland, where he was very active in not only promoting the veneration of the Immaculate Virgin, but also establishing a seminary, radio station, and several other organisations and publications. In 1914, he lost his father Julius, an ethnic German, when he was captured and hanged by the Russians for his part in fighting for an independent Poland. Maximilian kept busy working for Mary against the enemies of the Church. He helped the Immaculata Friars publish pamphlets, books and a daily newspaper. Their monthly magazine had over one million readers, and his radio station helped him reach many listeners. However, as for many saints, it was not all plain sailing. Maximilian suffered from tuberculosis, a condition that would plague him for the rest of his life. He never complained about his health – he regarded it as an opportunity to 'suffer for Mary'.

Maximilian's active ministry took him to Japan on a series of missions during the 1930s, where he founded a seminary and a monastery on the outskirts of Nagasaki. Ill health forced him to return to Poland in 1936, but not before he built his monastery. He decided to build it on the side of a mountain, which, according to Shinto beliefs, was not the right side to be in tune with nature. However, when the atomic bomb was dropped on Nagasaki in 1945, the monastery and the monks were saved, as the other side of the mountain took the main force of the blast. Maximilian never lived to witness the destruction of Nagasaki or Hiroshima, as his brutal death occurred four years earlier in Auschwitz.

Maximilian continued in religious life in the friary at Niepokalanów, the 'City of the Immaculata'. Before long, Niepokalanów had become one of the largest friaries in the world. In 1939 it housed 762 priests, brothers and novices. Niepokalanów went from strength to strength, making it a unique institution within Poland. The results of the work done there were becoming apparent. Priests in parishes all over the country reported a tremendous upsurge of faith, which they attributed to the literature emerging from Niepokalanów. However it was not to last. By 13 September, Niepokalanów was occupied by the Germans and most inhabitants, including Fr Maximilian, were deported to Germany for three months before being released back to Poland.

During their initial arrests under 'general suspicion', Maximilian reassured his fellow monks by saying,

> Courage, my sons. Don't you see that we are leaving on a mission? They pay our fare in the bargain. What a piece of good luck! The thing to do now is to pray well in order to win as many souls as possible. Let us then tell the Blessed Virgin that we are content, and that she can do with us anything she wishes.

Maximilian Kolbe would carry those sentiments to his grave.

His monastery and the wider community of Niepokalanów helped to hide, feed and clothe some three thousand Polish refugees, with an estimated one thousand five hundred of them being Jewish. His newspaper, *The Knight of the Immaculate*, continued to strongly criticise the Nazis. In February 1941, Maximilian was arrested by the Gestapo for hiding Jewish people. He spent a short time in the notorious Pawiak prison in Warsaw before being sent on his final journey to Auschwitz, where he was branded prisoner number 16670. What awaited the Poles who entered was outlined in the Führer's speech to the Wehrmacht High Command in August 1939:

> The object of war ... is to physically destroy the enemy. That is why I have prepared ... my 'Death Head' formations with orders to kill without pity or mercy, all men, women and children of Polish descent or language. Only in this way can we obtain the living space we need.

Maximilian's short time in Auschwitz was brutal. He was assigned to the exhausting work camp, which involved carrying heavy blocks of stone for the building of the crematorium wall. The work party was overseen by a convicted criminal known as 'Bloody Krott', so-called because of his penchant for annihilating prisoners and his ferocity towards Catholic priests. Father Kolbe, under the control of Krott, was bloodied and beaten half to death. Never once did he complain, but continued as best he could, hearing confessions and bringing solace to his fellow prisoners. On every occasion, he gave what food he could to others and encouraged all to pray for the conversion of the Nazis. He managed to write to his mother, reassuring her that all would be well, but in his heart he knew different. Father Kolbe told a fellow priest that he would survive the camp, but that he himself would not, as he had a mission to complete for the Immaculata.

After two months in the camp, he was transferred to another block from where a prisoner had attempted to escape. In reprisal for the escape, the SS selected ten men at random to be starved to death. One of the men selected, a Polish Army sergeant called Francis Gajowniczek, cried out, 'My poor wife and my children! I shall never see them again!' His pleas for mercy were ignored by the SS, but not by Fr Kolbe, who, in an unprecedented move, stepped forth to take his place. Eyewitnesses later recalled that it was a miracle that the priest wasn't shot on the spot. Boldly facing his executioners he said in flawless German, 'I want to make a request please ... I want to die in place of this prisoner ... I have no wife or children. Besides, I am old and not good for anything'. Father Kolbe used the Nazi argument that only the strong should live. His request was granted. Along with nine others, the priest was marched to the basement of the Death Block. A witness to Fr Kolbe's sacrifice remembered thinking, 'I've just seen a saint made'.[6]

An eyewitness to the events in the death bunker, Bruno Borgowiec, who was an assistant to the janitor and interpreter, retold the story:

> In the cell of the poor wretches there were daily loud prayers, the rosary and singing, in which prisoners from neighbouring cells also joined. When no SS guards were about, I went to the bunker to talk to the men and comfort them. Fervent prayers and songs to the Holy Mother resounded in all the corridors of the bunker. I had the impression I was in a church. Father Kolbe was leading and the prisoners responded in unison.

It took two weeks of starvation to end the lives of all but four of the prisoners. Deciding to speed things along, the SS injected the emaciated survivors with carbolic acid. Bruno Borgowiec continued:

> Father Kolbe was found sitting upright in the fetid cell. He held out his arm to receive the lethal injection. His body was described as clean and bright. The eyes were open and his face radiated serenity and purity.

His death on 14 August 1941 was on the feast day of the Assumption of the Blessed Virgin. Father Kolbe's remains were cremated at Auschwitz.

News of his death quickly spread from camp to camp. After the war, newspapers all over the world were filled with articles about this 'saint for our times'. Hundreds of oral testimonies were eventually collected by those who knew Fr Kolbe, including those interned at Auschwitz. Biographies were written, and everywhere there were claims of cures being brought about through his intercession. Two miracles were authenticated and Maximilian Kolbe was canonised in 1982 by fellow Pole, Pope John Paul II. Along with many religious and fellow Poles from around the world, Francis Gajowniczek was also present in St Peter's Square to honour the occasion. Francis never got the chance to thank Fr Kolbe in person, but he spent much of his life bearing witness to his sacrifice by travelling through Europe and America, giving talks about the Saint of Auschwitz. Francis Gajowniczek died in 1995, aged ninety-four.

Following the war, the Polish bishops sent an official letter to the Holy See claiming that Fr Kolbe's magazine had prepared the Polish nation to endure and survive the horrors of the war. The cell at Auschwitz where he died has been preserved and his statue is one of ten martyrs displayed above the west doorway of Westminster Abbey.

Father Maximilian Kolbe, a 'Child of Faith', kept his promise to Our Lady. He wore both of the crowns She offered and suffered martyrdom with all the qualities of a saint.

'Is That You, Aunt Harriet?'

The True Story That Inspired *The Exorcist*

The release of the movie *The Exorcist* in 1973, portraying the demonic possession of a young girl, resulted in mass hysteria. Some moviegoers fainted, some were frozen in their seats, and ambulances were on standby in others. It was considered one of the scariest movies ever made. Two Jesuits watched the movie in St Louis, Missouri, unimpressed by the hullabaloo. Fathers William Bowdern and Walter Halloran disliked the movie, but they gleaned satisfaction from knowing that it portrayed the reality of evil, albeit through a Hollywood filter. The true story that inspired the novel *The Exorcist* by William Peter Blatty, which was then made into a movie, took place in Missouri in 1949, when the Jesuits were called in to investigate strange goings-on in the Mannheim household.[7]

Robert Mannheim, an only child, was fourteen when his Aunt Harriet bought him a new boardgame. Harriet, a medium, often used the Ouija board to contact spirits. Robert was fascinated with the game and couldn't put it down. When his Aunt Harriet died in January 1949, he spent a lot of time trying to contact her using the board. Soon after, strange things began to happen. At first, the disturbances sounded like rats under the floorboards. Other times, a dripping tap could be heard. Robert's father ripped up floorboards, put down rat poison and removed wall panels to locate the source of the noise. Eventually it stopped. However, things soon deteriorated. Robert complained of squeaking shoes walking up and down on his bed. To console him, his mother and grandmother lay on the bed with him. They too heard feet marching up and down on his bed to the beat of drums. Exasperated, his mother called out, 'Is that you, Aunt Harriet?' All three felt a force press down on them, as loud knocking reverberated off the floor. His mother believed it was Harriet making contact over unresolved finances.

Matters only worsened. Wherever Robert went, objects flew into the air and chairs he sat on spun out of control. One night, responding to his screams, the family watched in horror as a wardrobe moved across the floor while Robert lay in bed. This alleviated his mother's suspicions that he was playing pranks. A number of doctors and psychiatrists were consulted. No one could find anything wrong with the boy. Their Lutheran minister prayed for deliverance, but considered diabolical possession outdated and best left to the Catholics. He and others believed the incidents were just adolescent pranks. However, he decided to take Robert to his own home so the boy could get some rest from what were considered to be mere household disturbances. Staying in the same room, the minister watched horrified as the boy was dragged under the bed by an unseen force, and bounced repeatedly against the bedsprings, leaving cuts on his face. Unable to deal with the diabolical, he informed Robert's parents, 'You have to see a Catholic priest. The Catholics know about things like this'.

The first priest to attempt the exorcism, Fr Hughes, was young and inexperienced. When he entered the hospital room where Robert was strapped to the bed, the boy – who appeared asleep – addressed him in Latin: 'O priest of Christ, you know that I am the devil. Why do you keep bothering me?' Ignoring the comment, Fr Hughes began the exorcism. Somehow, the boy freed his arm and dislodged a piece of bedspring. Plunging it into the priest, he sliced his arm from shoulder to wrist. The wound required over one hundred stitches. Father Hughes discontinued the exorcism, moved parishes and reportedly suffered a breakdown.

Robert's behaviour worsened. Back at his family home, shrieks and foul language bellowed from what neighbours renamed 'The Devil's House'. Shunned, the family moved in with relations. Like Aunt Harriet, their Lutheran relatives saw no harm in spiritualism. Once more, the Ouija board was consulted. It informed them that Harriet was the problem. Moving again, the family stayed with Catholic relatives so Robert could attend Catholic school, but scratches appeared on his body that spelled out 'No School'. At night, the house was besieged by demonic forces. As Robert tried to sleep, his bed shook violently and something unseen was frantically trying to scratch its way out of the mattress and the walls. Their Catholic relatives had seen enough. They turned to their church.

Having studied the case, the Jesuits were convinced the boy was possessed. Fathers Bowdern, the chief exorcist, Halloran and Bishop began the exorcism, with Fr Bishop taking meticulous notes. They witnessed scratch marks appearing on Robert's body, as though something was writhing under the skin. He shrieked in pain, as a demonic face appeared on his leg and the word 'Hell' appeared on his chest. When he awoke, he told the priests he dreamed he was battling a slimy, red devil, who was preventing him from leaving a burning pit. To help the family rest, the Jesuits moved Robert to the Alexian Brothers' Hospital. The first night of prayers went well. Father Bowdern allowed Robert to return to his relatives' home as he appeared to be settling down. Three days later, however, things worsened. Robert complained of his feet burning hot and cold. Disheartened, the family put him to bed and sent for the Jesuits. Robert went into a trance and began writing on bed sheets that the devil intended to depart, but the chilling messages ended in death threats to the priests.

To aid the exorcism, the family allowed Robert to be baptised a Catholic. In April of Holy Week, they drove him to the chapel. The boy went wild: 'So, you are going to baptise me!' he shouted in a chilling, guttural voice. Grabbing the wheel, he forced the car off the road. His uncle turned off the ignition but the key jumped out and landed near the backseat. Static noises came from the radio as Robert, with his hands around his mother's throat, attempted to throttle her. With superhuman strength, he continued his attacks on his father and uncle who managed to drag him from the car. The boy, kicking, screaming and cursing was forced into the church for baptism. After several hours of demonic resistance, the boy came to and accepted baptism. The next day, after nearly fifteen hours of rage, he finally accepted Holy Communion. Later, in his cousin's house, he attempted to throttle his Aunt Catherine. Once more, Fr Bowdern removed him to the Alexian Hospital. It was coming up to Palm Sunday and the Jesuits hoped for a breakthrough in the exorcism. The Brothers at the hospital answered knocks on their cell doors, only to find no one there. Screams and maniacal laughter rang throughout the hospital. The guttural voice of the demon informed the exorcists that the boy had to say a certain word before it would leave him in peace. But it would not say what the word was.

During the day, Robert's behaviour was somewhat normal. To get him away from the confines of the hospital, Fr Halloran and another Jesuit took him for a drive to a Jesuit estate. Looking at the Stations of the Cross, the boy went wild and ran to a nearby cliff, where he tried to throw himself over the edge. The priests struggled to get him into the car and back to the hospital. Proceeding with the exorcism, the boy, with eyes closed, cursed, spat, excreted, struggled, awakened, demanded food and threw it around the room. Then, one evening at 10.45 p.m., a strange quietness filled the room. A new voice came from the boy. It was clear and masterful. 'Satan! Satan! I am St Michael, and I command you, Satan, and the other evil spirits to leave the body in the name of Dominus. Immediately! Now!' Dominus. That was the word Fr Bowdern realised the demon said the boy would never speak. Then followed the worst period of resistance of the entire exorcism. The boy fought and blasphemed. Suddenly, he awakened, sat up and declared, 'He's gone!' The priests and Brothers wept with relief, all but Fr Bowdern. He was waiting for a sign that the demonic spirits had truly left. Robert told them his dream of the beautiful angel with flowing hair, who pointed to a burning pit where the devils stood. Robert felt the heat of the fire. The devil charged at the angel who spoke the word Dominus and the demons retreated to a cave prison with 'Spite' written across the bars.

The next day, Robert received Holy Communion. He said he had never felt as happy. He returned to his room in the hospital and took a nap. When he awoke, he asked the Brother where he was. He seemed to remember nothing of his ordeal. At that very moment, an explosion, like a gunshot was heard throughout the hospital. Brothers, nurses and staff rushed to the fifth floor to find Robert standing by his bed smiling. The unexplained explosion was the sign Fr Bowdern was waiting for. Often when demons are forced to leave a possessed person they will make a tremendous noise, signifying their anger at being forced out. After the exorcism, several Jesuits gathered in Francis Xavier Church. Suddenly, above the altar, they saw St Michael in a blaze of glory with a flaming sword in his hand. The ordeal was finally over.

Father Bowdern died in 1983, aged eighty-six. Father Bishop died in 1978, aged seventy-two. The young Fr Hughes recovered from his breakdown and remained in the priesthood, convinced of its tremendous power. He died in 1980, aged sixty-two. Robert Mannheim's parents converted to Catholicism. Robert himself never spoke publicly of Aunt Harriet or the story that inspired *The Exorcist.*

FEMALE
RELIGIOUS

Mother Mary Angelica

Founder of EWTN

When John Rizzo walked out on his wife Mae and five-year-old daughter Rita in 1928, he upended both their lives. These were the very difficult beginnings of a child who went on to become one of the world's most influential nuns, gracing two centuries and founding the Eternal Word Television Network (EWTN), the world's largest Catholic media outlet.

Mae and John divorced in 1930, leaving the insecure Mae to become more dependent on her young daughter. From the age of eleven, Rita recalled driving her mother's car to deliver starched clothes from their dry cleaning business in Ohio. Sometimes their customers paid, most of the time they failed to do so. It was a portent of what was to come, when Rita found herself navigating a much larger vehicle that spanned the globe.

Financial hardship forced Mae to return to her parental home in order to survive. As an adult, Rita recalled a lonely childhood. She was an underachiever, and religion only played a minor role in their lives. Rita's first encounter with the supernatural occurred as a young teenager. While crossing the road, she failed to see a car that almost knocked her down. She recalled, with clarity, two invisible hands picking her up and placing her safely on the centre island of the road. A bus driver told her he witnessed a miracle as he never saw anyone jump so high. This would not be Rita's only encounter with the divine.

A turning point came when, in her late teens, she was beset with severe stomach problems. Mae took her to see Rhoda Wise, a Catholic convert and mystic. Rhoda gave them a nine-day novena to the Little Flower. Rita was cured on the ninth day. Her brush with the supernatural helped her to endure future ailments that plagued her long religious life. She answered 'the call' in 1944 when she entered a cloistered order of Franciscan nuns in Cleveland, Ohio, much to the dismay of her mother. It would be a year before Mae could accept her daughter's decision.

Thirteen years after entering the convent, Rita, now Sister Angelica, received permission to establish a monastery in Birmingham, Alabama, which was a smouldering cauldron of racial and religious tensions. By 1961, Mae relocated to Alabama and eventually joined the monastery, taking the name Sister Mary David. Mother Angelica shouldered the burden of constructing and financing the monastery, and survived two separate gun attacks on the partially constructed building. Fundraising for Our Lady of the Angels Monastery was always on the agenda. Under the tutelage of the enterprising Angelica, the nuns made and sold fishing lures and, in addition, sales from dry roasted peanuts in 1968 helped clear the monastery debt.

Mother found a way to reach Catholics and non-Catholics through her evangelising parlour talks to various groups who sought her counsel. At the bishop's request, she went on speaking tours and, by 1971, found herself addressing a radio audience. Angelica's first book, *Journey Into Prayer* went to print in 1971. However, her writing came to a standstill when she was accused of splitting infinitives. With little education to fall back on, Angelica believed she had committed a literary crime. When informed that her readers would not recognise a split infinitive either, her courage returned and she quipped that she would write as one dummy to another. When one of her books was rejected by the printer, claiming a change in ownership, she started up her own printing press.[8] By 1976, the monastery was printing and distributing two hundred and fifty thousand books daily.

In 1978, on a speaking trip to Chicago, Angelica found the vehicle that would carry Catholicism to the masses: a Baptist-run television station. Believing that television was falling into the hands of the enemy, she seized her opportunity to broadcast alongside Evangelical Protestants. However, Angelica's sojourn into the airwaves was short-lived. Following a religious disagreement with a studio head, Angelica withdrew her programmes. She was informed that she would never work in television again. Like a red flag to a religious bull, Angelica was determined to start up her own television station. She did so – in a garage. By 1981, after financial struggles, technical problems and setbacks that would have deterred the most hardened of entrepreneurs, EWTN was about to be launched when the most devastating blow fell.

Concerns presented to Rome that a cloistered nun should be just that – cloistered – confined Mother to quarters and ended her speaking tours which had helped finance the cost of running EWTN. A further setback arrived with the delivery man who needed six hundred thousand dollars to unload the satellite dish. Mother informed him she did not have the money, but insisted he stay while she and the nuns pray in the chapel. Her prayers were answered when she received an unexpected donation of six hundred thousand dollars from a well-wisher. Angelica always believed she was on a mission from God, and that He would send her trials but He would be there to carry her through. Angelica's curfew was eventually lifted by a Vatican official who gave her permission to go back on the road. It later emerged that Rome approved of what EWTN was doing.

Mother's greatest challenge came from liberal American bishops who were starting their own TV network. When speaking to one bishop who was attempting to take control of EWTN, Mother screamed down the phone, 'I'll blow the darn thing up before you get your hands on it!' Angelica realised the insuperable damage the Church would suffer at the hands of the liberals. By 1983, Mother Angelica went live with her one-hour impromptu slot. For some twenty years she became religious agony aunt to the nation, delivering hard-hitting truths and advising listeners to amend their ways. Many found solace in her words and one of her early shows even saved a young man from suicide.

Her foray into the media came at an essential time for many traditional Catholics who were confused by the various interpretations of Vatican II. Recalcitrant bishops pushing for Church reform, and a cardinal denying transubstantiation saw Mother going headlong into religious battle. Angelica, according to one prelate, voiced what many orthodox were thinking but afraid to say, and paid a heavy price. However, now in her seventies, Angelica survived with the help of her ally in Rome, Cardinal Joseph Ratzinger. Mother Angelica had already met Pope John Paul II, who referred to her as 'Mother Angelica, the Grand Chief'.

However, her troubles were far from over and, once more, EWTN was under the microscope. Questions were raised as to who owned the network. If it belonged to Mother, it could be taken over by the local bishop. Although the investigating Vatican official wanted Mother to control EWTN, she and her trusted executives feared an episcopal coup, so Mother relinquished control.

The trials and tribulations Angelica faced took their toll on her health. She accepted everything God sent her, never praying for good health – just the ability to cope. When she was miraculously cured after forty-two years in back and leg braces, she believed it was to strengthen the faith of her staff and viewers. From sickness to health, Angelica endured. Following a stroke, she appeared before her audience and joked: 'Be not afraid. It's me.' Her courage saw sixty-five thousand letters flood the studio, many from stroke victims, thanking her for her courage and inspiration.

Bedridden for some fifteen years before her death at the age of ninety-two in 2016, Mother Angelica has been praised and criticised in equal measure. Her raison d'être was to save souls for Christ. With single-minded determination, and God on her side, she accomplished the impossible. The little girl from a troubled background touched the hearts of millions through her global network and brought Catholicism to the masses. She has been credited with helping to keep the Catholic Church in America from going under. For that, her legion of followers is eternally grateful.

Sister Clare Crockett

The Derry Girl

From a tender age, Clare Crockett had a burning ambition to be famous. Her mother Margaret called her the 'Drama Queen', as she hugged the limelight on every possible occasion. She excelled in school plays and her acting abilities brought her to the attention of a drama coach. She progressed into small acting parts and commercials from a young age. In 1997, aged fifteen, she was presenting a programme for young people on BBC Four. Two years later, the American channel Nickelodeon showed an interest in her. Her resume was not based on nepotism, but on natural talent.

Her love of all things theatrical took her into the world of theatre. She studied, wrote and directed theatre, always focusing on the goal of making it big. Her father Gerald spoke of her outgoing, larger-than-life personality. She had the ability to get on well with almost everyone she met. Her warm and friendly personality attracted people to her; she loved nothing more than being surrounded by a crowd.

According to Clare, her working-class Derry family were Catholic more for political reasons than from conviction. The Northern Irish community in which she grew up was divided along sectarian lines. Derry shared in the bloody history of the Troubles. Murders, bombings and shootings were part of everyday life, as the British establishment fought hard to maintain control of the six Ulster counties. Clare's mother Margaret once said in an interview that Clare, returning home from school one day, witnessed a British soldier being blown up. This was a sight nobody should ever have to see, but for communities in conflict situations, witnessing acts of violence was all too common. Clare managed to escape this environment by giving her all to acting.

In 1999, the parish youth group of St Columba's Church in Derry were visited by the Servant Sisters of the Home of the Mother. The Sisters invited a group of young people to join them in Spain. Clare was contacted by her friend Sharon, who invited her along. Clare, who was seventeen, was already smoking and drinking and did not receive the full message. She believed they were heading for a hedonistic holiday on the island of Ibiza. Sharon became ill before the trip to Spain and Clare reluctantly went along as it was, after all, a free holiday to sunny Spain. She found herself among a group of pilgrims, the youngest in their forties, all praying the rosary. She had stopped practising her religion in her early teenage years and when she was encouraged to join in the Holy Week festivities in Spain, she 'went along to get along'. On Good Friday, Clare sat at the back of the Spanish church, hoping on this rare occasion to avoid being noticed. She was told she would have to approach the altar and kiss the cross. She recalled standing in line to kiss the cross, which meant nothing to her, as the crucifixion had never been properly explained to her. As she bent to kiss the feet of the crucified Christ, she received the grace to fully understand that Christ had died for her sins and the sins of the world. It was an epiphanic moment that put her on the path to holiness and brought her closer to God's love. It was a love, she later recalled, that she had been searching for all her life. When the sufferings of Christ impacted on her mind and soul, she found herself weeping uncontrollably, as she realised her sins had contributed to His pain. At that point in her life, Clare resolved to change from a life of sin to one of holiness. However, it would not be without its struggles.

One of the Sisters who witnessed Clare weeping asked her if she was all right. Clare repeatedly blurted out, 'He loves me. He died for me. Why hasn't anyone ever told me this before?' Sister asked if she would like to see Fr Rafael Alonso, founder of the Home of the Mother convent. When Clare met with Fr Rafael, she told him she wanted to be a nun, like the Sisters. Clare was informed that she would have to return to Spain for instruction, which she agreed to do. She still had an overriding ambition to be famous, but she felt she could do both. She would become a famous nun. When she returned to Ireland the Sisters believed she would not return to Spain, but Fr Rafael disagreed – he saw something else stirring within the soul of the young woman.

Clare accepted an invite from Fr Rafael to join the Sisters on a pilgrimage to Rome. The Sisters were still sceptical about her vocation, as they witnessed what they thought was the behaviour of a young girl needing the limelight. Clare informed Fr Rafael that she intended to answer God's call to religious life, but the secular life and desire for fame and money was still strong within her. On her return to Ireland she once more went back to her old ways, partying and drinking to the point of sickness. It was during a particularly bad episode of drunkenness that she felt someone watching her being sick in the bathroom. She knew it was God and, in her heart, she heard his words, 'Why do you keep hurting me?' However, Clare was not yet ready to surrender herself to His will. The call of fame was still resonating within her.

Clare's next journey was to England, where she was starring in a film. It was a part she knew would open the door to further movie roles and success. Everything was organised – a personal assistant, make-up artists, a chauffeur, wining and dining in the best restaurants and staying in top hotels. It was all expenses paid – everything she ever wanted. She was on the threshold of stardom, but she felt empty. She knew what was missing. It was God. She summed up her life at that time, 'I lived very badly. I lived in mortal sin. I drank a lot, I smoked a lot, I began to smoke drugs. I continued with my friends, with my boyfriend. I continued in the same way. I didn't have the strength to break with all these things, because I didn't ask the Lord to help me.' So she made the final decision to shun the secular world and all its vainglory.

When she informed her family and friends of her decision to return to Spain to enter religious life, their reaction was one of disbelief and sadness. Her mother begged her not to go, not to turn her back on family and success. Clare knew to follow God. She would have to leave everything behind and trust in His infinite wisdom, which she did. Her spiritual transformation took time. Clare's manager often phoned the monastery, begging her to return with promises of stardom. He pleaded with her not to waste her life living as a nun. However, the old ways of wanting the limelight would eventually fade. No longer needing to be the centre of attention, Clare found time to listen to God. She put her trust in Him, knowing He would help her with the Spanish language and prepare her for religious life.

In 2003, Clare entered the novitiate and received the habit, denoting her willingness to live the life of a religious Sister. She took the required vows of chastity, poverty and obedience. Clare took a fourth vow to defend the Eucharist with her life, if necessary. In 2006, the Sisters founded a new community in Jacksonville, Florida. Clare was among the first of the Sisters to arrive. She went into the local school to instruct the children's catechism class. Her playful nature and exuberance was infectious and found a receptive audience in the young pupils. She was long remembered by teachers and pupils. One girl said of her, 'she made me want what she had – a great love for life and Christ'. She taught the children to have respect for the Eucharist, guiding them through her own example by showing reverence to the Mystical Body of Christ. Encouraging them to remain still for just three minutes in front of the monstrance, Clare told them that God would touch each and every one of them.

When it came time for the children to make their First Holy Communion, their mothers were almost moved to tears recalling the great devotion and respect the children showed towards the Eucharist. One teacher remembered the children proceeding with such reverence that she knew they were touched by the Holy Spirit. The parents attributed the children's piety to Sr Clare's ability as a catechist and her own devotion to Christ. She bestowed on the children a love for the rosary and the school's rosary club was a favourite with them. With Sr Clare in charge, she made prayer fun. The children's summer camp was not only entertaining for them, but also for the young Sisters helping Sr Clare. Her natural ability for acting and her sense of adventure ensured that the camps were fondly remembered by all.

On the suggestion of her Sisters and the youth group, who loved Ireland, Sr Clare found herself returning on pilgrimage to her homeland in 2010. The tour included a visit to Clare's family home in Derry. Her mother recalled that the small house had trouble accommodating the bus load that Clare brought home. People were to be found in every room, under the stairs, in the hall and out back. Clare was moved to tears reuniting with her family. It was the first time her family learned why she decided to answer the religious call. Her sister remembered it was still difficult for them to accept her move into religious life, but Clare's explanation helped them to understand her reasons. When one of the American girls asked Clare if she was not worried about leaving her family in such a war-torn city, Clare replied that Christ would take care of them.

When Clare took her final vows in 2010, Fr Rafael said her motto would be, 'Alone with Christ alone'. Clare was the only Sister to take final vows that year and, with her family in attendance, it was an emotional day for her. When her family witnessed Clare moved to tears, her sister worried it was tears of regret that she had turned her back on her dream of Hollywood. Clare later explained that her tears were ones of gratitude that she had finally been fully accepted into the convent of the Servant Sisters.

Her next sojourn took her to Valencia, Spain, where the Sisters opened a new house. Clare's willingness to always take on extra chores greatly impressed her superiors. Clare often said she signed a blank cheque for God and He could write whatever He wanted on it. The

Sisters' work took them into hospital care. Sister Clare encountered a man dying of AIDS. At first he wanted little to do with the Sisters, but Clare won him over. Regaling him with stories of her family in Derry, she made him feel comfortable with her. Eventually, Clare and the Sisters got him to make his confession and receive Communion. When Clare asked him what he liked about the Eucharist, he replied, 'It gives me life'. On one occasion, Clare asked if he would like to listen to music. He said: 'No. It will keep me away from my prayers.'

The Sisters were also involved in schoolwork, helping children from troubled backgrounds. Clare was a great source of encouragement to them. Her youthful enthusiasm was infectious and many of the girls remembered Clare with great affection. However, Clare's path through religious life was not all fun and games, as she suffered terribly from migraines. During one migraine attack, one of the Sisters found her being sick in the bathroom. Clare dismissed it, telling the Sister she would be fine and they had important work to do. She worked through her pain, always putting others before herself.

Sister Clare's last posting was in Ecuador, where the Sisters often trudged through waist-deep rivers to reach Indigenous tribes. The Sisters provided educational facilities for the impoverished children. The more difficult children were put under the care of Sr Clare, who always found a way to gain their trust. Class sizes were large and the heat was exhausting. Many of the Sisters welcomed a break after class finished. Clare however, found more activities to occupy her time by keeping the children amused. She said if she felt tired, she would be thinking of herself only and not of those she could help.

One particularly difficult class of young teenagers fell under the care of Sr Clare. They were considered underachievers who were not living particularly chaste lives. Through prayer, Clare reached out to them and won their trust. She spoke of their need to remain free from sin. They went on religious pilgrimage with her, eventually coming to appreciate Catholic teaching. Many of them recalled in interviews that it was Sr Clare who helped them achieve high grades in their studies. One young man said his spiritual life changed thanks to the example and encouragement of Sr Clare. The Sisters said of her that it was all or nothing. She did nothing by half measure and this was what she instructed the children to do – to give their all to studies and to God.

Once, during free time, one of the Sisters asked who among them would die first. Clare said she would die young. She hoped to die at thirty-three – the same age

Christ died. Her only worry was that she had not given enough to God. It was noted that she often preferred quiet time to be alone with God in front of the Eucharist. However, her need to give to the religious community often saw her in the front line, giving everything she had to those they served. In 2016, heavy rains flooded the entire area of Playa Prieta, including the school. The Sisters and the residents were devastated with the enormity of the damage done. It took a week of hard graft to get the area back to normality. Sister Clare was at the fore, saying, 'Let's save some souls'. She told them it was a great opportunity to offer up their struggles for the holy souls in Purgatory. At the end of a gruelling ordeal, one of the Sisters remembered the look on Sr Clare's face. She said it was a look of special beauty that came from within. The Sisters were asked were they not fearful that they could have died during the floods. Sister Clare asked what was there to be afraid of? Death, she said, would take her to her Lord, whom she desired to be with.

One evening in the Sister House, Clare, with guitar in hand, accompanied the young novices in their quarters singing the song 'I Prefer Paradise'. It was the last song Sr Clare would ever sing. A 7.8-magnitude earthquake struck Playa Prieta at 6.58 p.m. on 16 April 2016. At least 480 people died, with more than four thousand injured and 231 missing. Sister Clare and five others died when the Sister House collapsed, burying them beneath the rubble. Clare got her wish to die at the same age as Christ. She was seven months short of her thirty-fourth birthday. News of their deaths devastated the Sisters and the wider community.

The following month, Derry's close-knit community welcomed home one of its own. Sister Clare's remains were returned for burial. Father Graham, who officiated at the Mass that was attended by hundreds of mourners, described Sr Clare as 'a striking example of Derry womanhood'. The Bishop of Derry, Donal McKeown, told BBC Radio Foyle that he had been comforting Sr Clare's family.

The area in Ecuador where Sr Clare spent the last years of her young life has since been rebuilt. The local population speak of many conversions and special graces received through her intercession. Sister Clare was an inspiration to many. Books, films and documentaries highlight the life of this remarkable young woman who turned her back on fame. Her grave is visited by many people asking for her prayers. The brief religious life she chose inspired her own sisters to return to their religion. In secular life, Clare wanted to be famous and in religious life she wanted to be a famous nun. In death, Sr Clare Crockett, the Derry girl, achieved it all.

Mother Dolores Hart

From Hollywood Actress to Benedictine Nun

In 2016, Mother Dolores Hart celebrated fifty years of religious life at the Abbey of Regina Laudis in Connecticut. Mother tends to stand out from her Sisters thanks to the black beret she sports on top of her veil. She was given permission to wear the beret when, as a young nun, she informed Mother Benedict that her head was cold following the removal of her blond tresses. Her blond hair was not the only thing Dolores would part company with. While still in her early twenties, Dolores Hart turned her back on a promising Hollywood career to take religious vows.

Ever since childhood, Dolores longed to be a movie star like her father, Bert Hicks. Dolores described her teenage parents as beautiful people; her father had a strong resemblance to Clark Gable and her uncle was none other than Mario Lanza. When her mother was pregnant, Dolores' grandmother advised her to have a termination, as she considered the teenage parents too young to have a child. Thankfully, Dolores was born and spent the early years of her life living with her grandparents while her father pursued his career in Hollywood. The first encounter the young Dolores had with the movies was helping her projectionist grandfather. When he would fall asleep during the movie, Dolores was instructed to wake him up in time to change the reel. She remembered with glee that her grandfather would reward her with a nickel.

While living with her grandparents, Dolores – a non-Catholic – attended Catholic school. She was intrigued to see her friends receiving the 'bread' during Mass, and afterwards they would be given chocolate milk and cookies. Dolores longed for the chocolate milk and cookies more than anything and asked her teacher if she could receive the 'bread' so she would qualify for the treats. The teacher was delighted at Dolores's request to receive Communion and enrolled her, with her grandmother's permission, in the catechism classes. When Dolores asked her grandmother if she could become a Catholic, she didn't object as she considered it would do no harm. Dolores later recalled with humour that God reached her through chocolate milk.

At age eleven, Dolores finally got to join her parents in Hollywood. As a young teenager, she still longed to have an acting career. Her then boyfriend, Don Barbo, sent her photograph to studio heads. Paramount Pictures offered her a screen test and she landed her first movie role in 1957 when she starred alongside Elvis in the movie *Loving You.* She became the envy of women around the world when, during the movie, she gave Elvis Presley his first onscreen kiss. Dolores recalled with humour her first encounter with Elvis. Upon meeting the handsome young man for the first time on set, Dolores asked him what he did for a living. Not being involved in the music scene, she had never heard of him. She did, however, go on to star with Elvis in their second movie *King Creole*, released a year later.

Dolores went on to make six more films, including *Francis of Assisi*, where she played the part of St Clare, who founded the Order of Poor Clares. While filming the movie, Dolores met Pope John XXIII through a contact. She introduced herself to the pope as an actress playing the part of St Clare. She recalled the pope smiled at her and, in Italian, told her: 'You are not playing Clare, you are Clare.' Dolores was confused by this and when she asked her friend what the pope meant, she was told that maybe the pope was discerning. Dolores had not yet contemplated a religious life, but it was not far off.

Her first sojourn with the religious came in 1959 after an exhausting stint on Broadway when she starred in *The Pleasure of His Company*, which won her a Tony Award for Best Featured Actress. Looking for a tranquil hideaway, a friend suggested she try the cloistered convent of Regina Laudis in Connecticut. Dolores was a little dubious about going in among nuns, but as soon as she set foot on convent grounds, she felt God call her to religious life. She felt so at home among the nuns that she asked the Reverend Mother if she could stay. Mother Superior advised her to return to Hollywood, make a few more movies and come back to the convent when she was a little older.

While still acting, and engaged to Don Robinson, Dolores found herself walking in two worlds. Don realised she was preoccupied with her desire to enter the convent and he told her she had to decide between the convent or married life. They both arranged to meet with the archbishop's representative in Los Angeles to discuss Dolores becoming a Benedictine nun. Dolores laughed when she reflected on their meeting with the prelate.

He informed Dolores that the Benedictines were a self-sustaining convent. He asked Dolores if she could cook, keep house and grow food. When she informed him that, as a busy actress, she had a lady who did all of that for her, the priest looked at Don. With sincerity, he informed Don that Dolores was not cut out to be a nun and questioned if she would make it as a wife.

Many within Hollywood could not understand Dolores's desire to turn her back on a promising and lucrative career. She was considered to be Hollywood's next Grace Kelly. However, unlike Kelly, who turned her back on Hollywood to become a princess, Dolores left to become a cloistered nun. The white dress she wore on the day of her profession was made by her good friend Maria Cooper, daughter of Gary Cooper. Dolores said it was Maria who guided her through Hollywood and advised her on the places to avoid.

Dolores described her early years in the convent as similar to being locked in a closet and forgotten. However, she accepted the seismic change in her life as she knew this was what God wanted for her. She got to keep her love of theatre alive when she founded The Gary The Olivia open-air theatre with her good friend Patricia Neal, now deceased. The theatre gives yearly performances in the grounds of the convent. In 2015, her acclaimed autobiography *The Ear of the Heart* had its third printing. In 2012, HBO made a documentary about Mother's life, entitled *God is the Bigger Elvis*. The production was nominated for an Oscar.

Dolores's artistic talents didn't end when she left Hollywood, she merely transferred them to the convent where she is busier than ever, serving the Lord.

Sister Blandina

The Fastest Nun in the West

When Rose Marie Segal left the Italian village of Cicagna at the age of four to emigrate to America with her family, she had no idea that her love for God would not only take her into convent life at the age of sixteen, it would also land her in a world of gun slingers, desperadoes and lynch mobs.

Joining the Order of St Elizabeth, Ann Seton's Sisters of Charity in Cincinnati in 1866, she took the name Sr Blandina. Her older sister, Maria, also joined and took the name Sr Justina. Sister Blandina was first appointed to teach in schools in Ohio. After spending several years teaching, she was informed she was being sent to Trinidad. When Blandina first heard this she thought she was being sent to the Caribbean. It was only later she was informed that it was Trinidad, Colorado, home to outlaws and ruffians.

Undaunted, the twenty-two-year-old nun made the dangerous journey and joined four other nuns living in a simple house in the dusty town. Before long, the Sister of Charity found herself embroiled in Colorado's lynch laws. Asked to intervene in a shooting that left one man dying and his assailant facing summary justice at the hands of a rope-swinging mob, Sr Blandina bravely made her way to the deathbed of the injured man. She begged the man to forgive his assailant. Sister Blandina could not bear to think of the man dying with hatred in his heart. To encourage him towards forgiveness, she made him a promise that his attacker would face a judge and jury rather than a lynch mob. Reluctantly, the man agreed. The Sister's next move required even more daring. Asking permission from the sheriff to accompany the accused man to the deathbed of his victim so he could receive forgiveness, the Sister took one of the first steps towards challenging Colorado's lynch laws by encouraging the townsfolk to abandon summary justice and instead try criminals before a judge and jury. Hesitantly, the sheriff agreed. His serious concern was that the mob would lynch the three of them once they stepped outside the jail house.

With her customary determination and unshakable faith, the Sister walked the sheriff and his prisoner through the angry mob to the bedside of the wounded man. Receiving forgiveness, the prisoner returned to jail unharmed. He eventually faced a judge and jury and received a life sentence for murder.

This one particular episode in the Sister's colourful life inspired a thirty-minute TV programme in 1966 called *The Fastest Nun in the West*. However, Sr Blandina's exploits in the Wild West did not end here. Her next encounter was with an outlaw called William Bonney, known as Billy the Kid. Some historians don't believe that Sr Blandina ever met the notorious Billy the Kid, but instead she met another desperado, William LeRoy, also known as Billy the Kid. Whoever the outlaw was does not detract from the Sister's direct intervention which saved the town's doctors from being scalped. One of Billy the Kid's gang members had been accidentally shot and left to die. The town's doctors refused to treat him, but Sr Blandina did not. Rushing to the aid of the injured man, she dressed his wounds and brought him food and water. When Billy learned of the doctor's refusal to help his fellow gang member, he rode into town threatening to ride off with their scalps. Fortunately for them, Billy stopped by to thank the nun for her help. Telling her it would be his pleasure to return the favour, the Sister wasted no time. Taking the young outlaw by the hand, she told him the only favour he could do for her was to leave the doctors with their scalps. Reluctantly, Billy agreed and rode out of town.

Sister's next encounter with Billy the Kid was during a stagecoach journey. Hearing that Billy was nearby, the passengers armed themselves. The Sister told them to put their guns away and said her rosary. When the robber got near the stagecoach, Sr Blandina looked up at him. Each recognising the other, Billy raised his hat to the nun who saved his friend and rode off. In her letters to the Sister House in Cincinnati, Sr Blandina described the young outlaw. His eyes were blue-grey, his complexion rosy and he had the air of a little boy.

Sister Blandina carried out active ministry in the service of Our Lord. Her twenty-odd years in the outback of Colorado and Santa Fe, New Mexico, were fondly marked by those who remember her for her charitable works. During her time in New Mexico, she and the Sisters of Charity gave the region its first hospital and public school, and contributed to the first nursing school for X-ray and laboratory technicians, later known as St Vincent.

The pioneering Sisters also established the first blood bank in New Mexico. By 1883, the St Joseph Healthcare

System included three acute-care hospitals and a rehab hospital. Sister Blandina was actively involved in social issues of the day and found herself helping Native Americans, the marginalised, and immigrant women and children. Wherever injustice was to be found, so too was Sr Blandina. Her good works and generosity inspired many to convert to the Catholic faith.

At the age of eighty-one, she travelled to Rome to petition Pope Pius XI in the cause of Sr Elizabeth Seton. In 1809, Mother Seton founded The Sisters of Charity of St Joseph's in Maryland, the first community of religious women to be established in America. In 1933, Sr Blandina retired to the Motherhouse in Cincinnati. Her letters and journals were published under the title, *At the End of the Santa Fe Trail*. The book is described as a valuable addition to the story of women in the Wild West. Sister Blandina died in 1941 at the age of ninety-one. In 2014, the Archbishop of Santa Fe, Michael Sheehan, called for her canonisation. If the cause is successful, the Sisters of Charity will be giving New Mexico yet another gift.

Sister Katharine Drexel

Philadelphia's Saint in the Making

The Drexel mansion was an imposing edifice on Walnut Street in downtown Philadelphia. The family head, Francis Anthony Drexel, was a prominent investment banker and one of America's wealthiest men. He was also a devout Catholic. He had a chapel built in his mansion and often prayed there after finishing work. His wife, Hannah, died in 1858, shortly after giving birth to their second daughter Katharine Mary, who was born during the apparitions at Lourdes. Following Hannah's death, Katharine and her sister, Elizabeth, were cared for by their aunt and uncle, Ellen and Anthony Drexel.

When the girls' father remarried in 1860, he and his new wife, Emma Bouvier, brought the girls home to live with them. Emma bore Francis a third daughter, Louisa, born in 1863. The girls were brought up to share their father's philanthropic ideals. Three times a week, the Drexel mansion threw open its doors to receive the poor and destitute. Food, clothing and rent assistance was distributed from the mansion. Those too proud to ask for assistance, the family discretely sought out and offered financial aid. Emma Drexel taught the girls that kindness may be unkind if it leaves a sting. It was a lesson not lost on the sisters, and one to which Katharine would dedicate her religious life.

Katharine and her sisters received a first-class education in languages, literature, philosophy, music and painting. They were educated at home by private tutors. When the girls were young, the family did what only the wealthy could afford to do – they toured Europe and various parts of America. However, the girls were not brought up to believe that their vast wealth was strictly for them. Their father often instructed his daughters that their wealth had been entrusted to them and had to be used to help those less fortunate than themselves.

At fourteen, Katharine was already a serious young girl with a strong spiritual awakening. At this tender age, she made the acquaintance of Fr James O'Connor who became a spiritual guardian and helped shape the direction her life would eventually take. As was the standing at the time, on turning twenty, Katharine was introduced to Philadelphia's high society. Given their status and wealth, Katharine and her siblings were considered a good catch. This fact was not lost on their father. Francis Drexel made provision in his will that his daughters would inherit his vast fortune. If they married, the money would pass only to their children. If they stayed single or produced no children through marriage, then, on their deaths, the fortune would be given to charities. However, for Katharine, high society held no allure. She found the experience rather boring and meaningless.

The Drexel sisters suffered a double loss when, in 1885, their parents died within a short space of time of each other. Katharine was still in her twenties and had watched helplessly as her beloved stepmother, Emma, suffered the ravages of cancer before succumbing to the disease. Katharine realised that all their great wealth could do nothing to prolong the life of their mother. One-tenth of their father's fortune – an estimated four hundred million dollars in today's terms – was left to charities and the rest was split between the sisters. Feeling the great burden of this wealth but not sensing the benefits, Katharine questioned what she could do with the money and, more importantly, what she could do with her life.

The answer to her question presented itself in the form of two clerics, Bishop Marty and Fr Stephan. The priests informed Katharine of their involvement in the Catholic Indian Mission, which had been established to help poor Indigenous people. Katharine had seen for herself the plight of the Native Americans when she and her family visited the western states shortly before her father's death. Katharine gave generously to the missionary priests and even travelled west to see the benefits of her donation. This would not be the last generous contribution the Drexel sisters would make to worthy causes.

Still reeling from the deaths of their parents, the sisters once more visited Europe. They were received at the Vatican by Pope Leo XIII. Katharine spoke passionately of her desire to see a religious order established to administer to the needs of the Native Americans. The pope astounded Katharine when he suggested that she should be that missionary light, the one to establish her own order of nuns. When Katharine mentioned this to her spiritual director, he questioned how a privileged, upper-class young woman could endure the rigours of missionary life. However, he eventually reconciled to the idea and Katharine entered the Sisters of Mercy, Pittsburgh, in 1889. Her decision rocked Philadelphia social circles so much so that one newspaper carried the headline: 'Miss Drexel Enters a Catholic Convent – Gives Up Seven Million.' Unphased by it all, Katharine went on to establish the Sisters of the Blessed Sacrament for Black and Native American people. By 1894, the Sisters had established their first Native American school among the Pueblo people of Santa Fe.

In 1957, Joseph Skye became the first Native American to graduate from Xavier University in New Orleans. The university was the first of its kind in America to offer advanced studies to young Indigenous and Black people. Skye never met Mother Katharine, but he never tired of hearing stories about her from Irish-born Sr Celine. Sister told her pupils about the millionairess from Philadelphia who befriended Chief Red Cloud of the Great Sioux Nation. With enthusiasm, she recounted the missionary zeal of their benefactor who financed churches, missions and schools all across America from her personal fortune. Sister Katharine has been described as one of America's most influential women; she was ahead of her time in demanding civil rights for all. In the true spirit of the Drexel family, her younger sister, Louise, contributed millions to similar causes. Their eldest sister, Elizabeth, died in 1890 in premature childbirth, one year before Catherine formed the Sisters of the Blessed Sacrament.

In 1935, Sr Katharine suffered a heart attack. Ordered to take things easy, she spent the next twenty years praying in front of the Blessed Sacrament for the success of her Order. Living up to her vow of poverty, she mended her own shoes and kept pencil stubs to reuse. Katharine died in 1955, but her work goes on and her community is worldwide. She was canonised by Pope John Paul II in 2000 after a cure for deafness was attributed to her intercession. Katharine Drexel is the second recognised American-born saint – the first being Elizabeth Ann Seton, who was canonised in 1975.

Sister Katharine Mary Drexel established schools, churches and missionary centres in twenty-one states throughout America, with a sharp focus on caring for the educational and social needs of Black and Indigenous people. Katharine had found a way to dispose of their family's vast wealth. In doing so, she lived up to the ideals of her father, an international banker with a social conscience that inspired his daughters.

Saint Brigid

Queen of the Gael

One of the most popular of the Irish saints is, strangely enough, shrouded in myth and legend. It is believed that Brigid was born in AD 450. Her mother, Broicsech, was brought to Ireland as a slave. One source claims Broicsech, a Christian, was brought from Portugal by Irish sea raiders. The sea crossing for the captives was very dangerous and those who survived knew little of the fate that awaited them in the strange new land on the western outskirts of Europe.

Brigid's mother was sold to Dubhthach, a young pagan chieftain of Leinster. Although Dubhthach was already married, he went on to father a child with Broicsech and he called his new daughter Brigid, after a pagan goddess.

The early story of Brigid is associated with Faughart in Co. Louth, although her prowess and reputation spread throughout the island of Ireland. Growing up as the daughter of a slave, Brigid seems to have displayed few if any subservient qualities. By all accounts she displayed a strong, independent spirit. As a free woman and a valued member of her father's clan, Brigid resisted all attempts by her father to have her marry a suitor of equal standing, in the hope that he would consolidate power between his kingdom and a neighbouring one. Much to his chagrin, she informed her father that she wanted to enter religious life. She was said to have possessed great beauty and that placed her in high demand as a wife. One account tells us that to discourage suitors, Brigid prayed to God to take away her beauty. Her prayers were answered when her face was scarred by the pox. However, the disfigurement only lasted until she entered religious life. When she made her religious vows to St Macaille, Bishop of Croghan, Co. Offaly, the scarring vanished.

It is believed that Brigid was around fifteen or sixteen when she became a religious Sister. An early version of Mother Teresa, she travelled the land visiting various settlements helping the sick, the poor and the outcasts. She prayed the animals would survive the harsh Irish winters, thus ensuring that the settlements would have food to eat and milk to drink. Not content with charitable work alone, Brigid sought to establish a church in Co. Kildare, a busy intersection at that time that Brigid knew would attract a lot of people.

In AD 470, Brigid and a small group of nuns arrived in Kildare in the hope of building their church. Brigid approached the local hierarchy, imploring them for permission to build a monastery for the nuns. Because of her young age, the local bishop was inclined to dismiss the girl, believing her religion and adherence to Patrick to be a mere fad. However, after spending time in her company, he came to realise that she was a sincere and devoted disciple. After winning over the bishop, Brigid's next move was to ask the local chieftain for land on which to build. After refusing several requests from the young nun, the chieftain accompanied Brigid out to the spot where she wanted to build her monastery. Legend has it that, hoping to best her, the chieftain told her to throw her cloak on the earth. 'Wherever it covers,' he told her, 'shall be your land to build upon.' Brigid dutifully obliged and, with complete trust in God, cast her cloak on the ground. The cloak kept spreading out in every direction. By the time it came to a halt, Brigid had secured two thousand hectares of land. The chieftain was so astounded that he gave her the land and converted to Christianity. The land today is known as the Curragh of Kildare. The locals refer to it as St Brigid's pastures.

Brigid's monastery was called The Church of the Oak. It was built beneath a large oak tree, close to a Celtic pagan shrine dedicated to the goddess Brigid was named after. Brigid built two religious houses for nuns and monks. She invited the hermit, St Conleth – who is believed to have come from Co. Wicklow – to act as abbot to the monks. The two religious houses, although separate, acted together to further the faith throughout the land and administer to the populace.

Brigid operated in a world governed by Celtic chieftains, feuding clans and warring settlements. Despite this, her strength of character, indomitable spirit and strong presence set her apart. News of the religious women spread throughout Ireland, and many young women sought them out to ask for advice and guidance. Brigid's convent increased in number as more and more young women decided to take the veil. Brigid was known as a peacemaker and was often asked to intervene and settle disputes among various factions. The nuns became known as 'women who turned back the streams of war' – no easy feat in a warrior society.

It is believed that Brigid met with St Patrick, learned from him and, like him, evangelised not only in Ireland but further afield. When the Irish monks and missionaries left their native land, they carried with them the stories of Patrick and Brigid. She was seen as a role model for young European women. It is believed, but not proven, that St Brigid of Sweden may have been influenced by St Brigid of the Gael. In Ireland, her light never dimmed. It is said there are more places named after Brigid than Patrick.

There are hundreds of holy wells throughout Ireland dedicated to St Brigid. Saint Brigid's Holy Well, situated in the grounds of the Black Abbey in Co. Kildare, is believed to possess healing properties. It is a popular place of pilgrimage for locals and tourists alike. County Kildare is also home to the Brigidine Sisters, which was founded on 1 February – the feast day of St Brigid – in 1807 by Daniel Delany, Bishop of Kildare and Leighlin. The Brigidine Sisters are the only order of nuns dedicated to St Brigid. They carry on the yearly tradition of making the St Brigid's cross. The cross, we are told, originated with the saint herself. Brigid was asked to visit the deathbed of a dying chieftain in Kildare. While praying at his side, Brigid picked rushes off the floor and began forming them into a cross. The chieftain enquired as to what she was doing. When she explained the religion of Patrick to him, the man accepted baptism.

Long associated with the seasons and agriculture, which are vital to the Irish, Brigid's feast day is the first day of spring. Farmers often look for favourable weather signs for planting around this day. In the 1940s, the museum and heritage centre in Castlebar, Co. Mayo, conducted an extensive survey into Irish customs and traditions associated with Brigid. Thousands of letters flooded in. They spoke of the Brideog doll, or Biddy, which was a straw effigy of St Brigid that was carried by children known as the Biddy Boys, who would travel from house to house. They would call out:

This is Biddy dressed in white
Give her a penny for this dark night.
She is deaf, she is dumb
For God's sake, give her some.

In other parishes, the custom would be for the girls to go out and gather rushes. On their return, they would knock three times on their family door, asking if they were ready to receive St Brigid. The family would kneel in prayer, asking Brigid to protect, home, family and livestock. They would cook a meal of the food they wanted protected. For many, it would be a plate of potatoes. It was often possible to tell how many years a family occupied a house. Each year, a new St Brigid's cross would be made and placed alongside the others in the rafters or out in the byre.

One parish in Co. Clare has a collection of St Brigid's crosses going back generations. One cross with three legs depicts devotion to Brigid in the Isle of Man. The parish has an authentically dressed Brideog doll made of straw. They display it alongside St Brigid's girdle, a straw circle decorated with crosses that symbolises Christology. When the girdle is placed over a person, they are protected on all sides by Christ. The girdle was carried by the boys of the village who would visit each and every house.

It is believed that St Brigid died in AD 525, aged seventy-five. Her body initially resided in the cathedral in Kildare. It is claimed she was later exhumed and buried in Downpatrick, Co. Down, alongside St Patrick and St Colmcille. Other accounts tell us that her skull was brought to St John the Baptist Church, Portugal, by two Irish noblemen.

Fifteen hundred years have passed, but, like St Patrick, St Brigid will live forever in the hearts and minds of the Irish. Perhaps our greatest tribute to her comes from the childhood prayer, remembered by Sr Rita of the Brigidine Sisters:

Brigid, Mary of Ireland
Ask for us all today
The courage to do God's bidding
Whatever the world may say.
The grace to be strong and faithful
The grace to be firm and true
The grace to be faithful always
To God, God's Mother and you!

THE LEGION
OF MARY

Frank Duff

Founder of the Legion of Mary

Described by Mao Zedong as 'Public Enemy Number One' due to the spread of his missionary zeal throughout Communist China, Frank Duff was a saviour to the destitute and an inspiration to his legion of followers. Born in 1889 to a prosperous family, Frank's journey would take him from civil servant to social worker on a mission from God.

Frank's parents, both from Trim in Co. Meath, were civil servants. His mother was among the first to pass the English civil service exam when it was opened to women. She was appointed to London but returned to Ireland when an opening appeared within the Dublin civil service. Frank suffered from typhoid, the same illness that killed his father in 1918. While the family were considered wealthy, due to bad investments, Frank had to skip university and go to work to help support the family. In 1908, in his nineteenth year, he joined the civil service. The eldest of seven children – two who died young – Frank passed through the educational system of Belvedere College, run by the Jesuits, before finishing at Blackrock College.

True to his upbringing, Frank was a deeply religious man. He recalled, with humour, being referred to as 'the local mad man of Dublin' – a reference to his early days when he often prayed the rosary outside houses of ill repute. He became so well known, and to a large extent respected, in the red-light districts of Dublin that it aided his endeavours to eventually have them closed down. Frank visited the Lancashire Regiment, stationed in Dublin, prior to Irish independence. He would carry the brown scapular medals, distribute them to the soldiers and encourage them to pray to Our Lady for spiritual guidance. Many of the soldiers were receptive to the proposition, and, on one occasion, seventy of them asked the priest for confession.

In 1913, Frank joined the Society of St Vincent de Paul. It not only deepened his faith, it gave him a greater appreciation of the suffering and deprivation of a great many of the populace. It would help transform his ministry from part-time volunteer to full-time lay apostolate, working for the greater good of the marginalised. He was greatly influenced by the writings of St Louis-Marie de Montfort, who inspired true devotion to the Blessed Virgin. Realising that Our Lady is vital to salvation history, Frank established a new Catholic lay organisation in 1921, known as the Legion of Mary. Along with a group of Catholic men, women and early spiritual directors, Fr Michael Toher and Fr Creedon of the Dublin Archdiocese, the first executive committee of the Legion, known as the praesidium, was formed in Myra House, Francis Street, Dublin. At the initial meeting, Frank informed those present that due to the power of the Holy Spirit, the Legion would transverse the world. Frank recalled, with humour, that the assembled body found his remarks so hilarious, that it was some time before they stopped laughing. However, his words were prophetic – a legion of laity, inspired by Frank, would indeed transverse the globe.

Eventually leaving the civil service in 1932, Frank channelled his energies to full-time Legionary work. He compiled the Legion Handbook, which defined the Legion as a voluntary lay body that was at the disposal of the bishops and priests for the welfare of the Church.

It was not always seen that way by the early archdiocese, who viewed it with suspicion. They were wary of the laity having too much say in Church affairs. However, Frank never envisaged it as a hindrance but as an aid to spreading the Gospels through the laity. It would be the 1960s before the Dublin bishopric looked favourably on the Legion, after Frank was praised by Pope Paul VI at the Vatican Council. The pope had such great respect for the Legion that he invited Frank to attend the Second Vatican Council as a lay observer.

In the early days, Frank made excursions to England, Rome and America, promoting the work of the Legion. For the most part he was home-based, putting much of his energies into helping prostitutes in Dublin. Frank recalled in interviews the early days of the Legion, visiting the notorious red-light district of Montgomery Street, or 'Monto' as it was commonly known. Frank initially worked with two female social workers, visiting the women and girls who staffed the brothels. He heard sad tales of their lives. They tearfully told him they hated what they did, but no one else would employ them. Father Creedon offered to pay the madam of one house maintenance on the promise she would not put the women back on the streets. The Legion needed a more permanent solution. In 1923, they established the Santa Maria hostel as a refuge and rehabilitation centre for the women and girls. It was a great success. Conversions were made, women left the streets, married or found different employment.

However, not all were so lucky. Frank was informed that one young girl named Mary Tate was dying and was asked to visit her. He and a female social worker found her seriously ill in one of the houses. They took her to hospital in Townsend Street, an old venereal hospital, where she lived for six weeks. She informed them that she no longer wanted to live – she was ready to die. Her last request was to ask the ward to pray the rosary with her. Mary was buried in Glasnevin Cemetery, attended by many of the women she worked with in Monto. It was not the last time Frank would ever hear of her. Some time later, when he visited Mullingar, he mentioned Mary. He was astounded to find out that Mary had disappeared from Mullingar, her hometown, when she was eighteen. The people in the area often wondered what became of her. Frank brought closure to the mystery of Mary's disappearance.

Attempting to clean up Monto wasn't all plain sailing. Frank was threatened on various occasions and once he was physically attacked by a knife-wielding man. He managed to stave off the attack and rendered the man a blow that completely disarmed him. Frank, who was slight in stature, believed a higher power was looking after him. On another occasion, he was confronted by a bouncer who was sent in to remove them from one of the houses. Frank described the bouncer as looking like Rudolph Valentino, the 1920s matinee idol. His sister, Victoria, worked in the brothel. Frank spoke to both of them. The young man told Frank he was a shoplifter by day and he worked in the red-light district at night. He agreed that his life was bad but didn't know how to change it. Frank persuaded him to join the retreats in Rathfarnham, which he did. A local priest got him fixed up with a job in Liverpool. Years later he returned to Ireland a changed man. He informed Frank that he never returned to his old life. Through Legion work and retreats, Frank managed to free many women from a life on the streets. Monto eventually imploded thanks to the efforts of the Legion of Mary. The poor were moved into the empty houses vacated by the prostitutes.

In 1927, the Legion opened a hostel for destitute men. Regina Ceoli hostel was also established to accommodate destitute women and their children. Frank believed that mothers and their children should be kept together and opposed sending illegitimate children into industrial schools. He confessed to having a great love for children and believed if he had ever married, he would spend too much time with his children and less time on Legion work. When asked why he never married, he once quipped that it was 'better to keep a dozen women in hopeful anticipation than make one woman miserable all her life'.

Quiet and unassuming, Frank Duff claimed credit for very little. Every success the Legion enjoyed was put down to the power of the Holy Spirit and the Queen of Heaven. As a daily communicant, he spent three to four hours a day in prayer and read the Divine Office. For forty-nine years of his life, until he turned seventy-four, Frank made the annual, gruelling pilgrimage to Lough Derg in Co. Donegal. In his later years he remained an active Legionary, working as a councillor after stepping down as Legion president.

Frank Duff died peacefully at home in November 1980. The President of Ireland, government ministers and the people of Ireland turned out in force to pay their last respects. The chief concelebrant, Cardinal O'Fiaich, described Frank as a man of personal charm and unshakable courage. He also referred to Frank as the Irishman of the century. In 1996, Dr Desmond Connell introduced the cause for Frank's canonisation. The Legion he so loved, which has spread to almost two hundred countries and has some four million active members, may yet have its first saint.

Alphonsus Lambe

From Legion of Mary to Servant of God

When their youngest son Alphonsus was born on 24 June 1932, the feast of St John the Baptist, Kate and Timothy Lambe could scarcely imagine that their delicate child would one day leave an indelible mark on South America as a Legion of Mary envoy. It would be a short but propitious life for Alfie. In the service of God, Alfie, like St John the Baptist, evangelised with a boundless streak of zealous energy that took many by surprise.

The youngest of eight children, Alfie was prone to fainting fits. His family were hard-working and deeply religious. His mother's favourite, Alfie informed his parents that he wanted to enter the Christian Brothers. While it came as no surprise to his family, it would be three years before the sixteen-year-old Alfie Lambe was given permission by his parents to enter the novitiate in Dublin. His mother accompanied him on the train journey from their home in Tullamore, Co. Offaly. In 1948, Alfie – along with forty other young men – joined the Brothers. Alfie was given the name Brother Ignatius. He remembered it as being the happiest day of his life. His fellow novitiates were struck by his piety and deep devotion to Our Lady.

While in the Christian Brothers, Alfie was drawn to the work of the Legion of Mary, started twenty-seven years previously by Frank Duff. Little did he know then that the Legion would soon beckon. Alfie's fainting fits continued and proved a worry for the Brother Superior. The decision was taken to send Alfie home in the hope he would make a complete recovery, and eventually return to the Brothers to finish his training. Alfie was devastated by the news. It was quickly followed by another blow when he learned of the death of his father.

Alfie's arrival home was one of mixed emotions. In one way, he was happy to be back in the bosom of his family, but the loss of his father and the longing for religious life never quite subsided. Alfie found work in the packing department of Salts Ireland Ltd, later known as Tullamore Yarns. After two years, the company closed. The turning point in Alfie's life came when his brother Jack invited him to attend a meeting of the Legion of Mary. Jack, himself an active member, would inadvertently be the one to help his young brother find his true calling in life.

Alfie threw himself into Legion work. No task was too great or too small. Working all hours, Alfie spread devotion to Our Lady throughout the rural parishes of Ireland. His sister Kathleen said that he would set off on his bicycle early on a winter's evening and return at midnight soaked to the skin with little or nothing to show for his efforts. However, the next night he would set off again to another parish, often carrying a portable altar on his bike, to continue Legion work. Eventually, he moved to Dublin where he worked full time for the Central Council. Three years later, at just twenty-one, he was appointed the youngest ever Legion Envoy. Alphonsus Lambe was about to take South America by storm. Frank Duff would later say of Alfie, 'The Brothers' loss was the Legion's gain'.

Having thrown himself into learning Spanish, Alfie accompanied his good friend Seamus Grace to South America as Legion Envoy. Both men landed in New York in 1953 before flying to their final destination, Bogota, Colombia. Bogota was not Alfie's final stop, but the first of many. Spending their first year there, both men were eased into their new role by a fellow Legionary, Joaquina Lucas. Under her tutelage, Alfie became proficient in Spanish and by the end of the year, he was ready to go it alone.

Alfie bade a final farewell to Seamus before journeying to Ecuador to begin the arduous task of spreading the work of the Legion of Mary. Conditions in the region were described as deplorable and Alfie was a welcome visitor. The bishop wasted no time employing Alfie's formidable talents to help improve conditions for the people. Alfie established two branches of the Legion with the promise of more to follow. The bishop was so impressed that he invited Alfie to address a meeting of the hierarchy, who responded positively. With Alfie's enthusiasm, the new Legionaries of Ecuador responded in kind. By learning the ways of the Legion and attempting to emulate Alfie in spreading the faith, they gave their time and money, and soon branches of the Legion began to spread throughout the entire country. The new praesidia reflected every walk of life. The wealthy and privileged, as well as the poor and outcast all united under the Legion banner.

Soon Alfie's reputation spread to the surrounding frontiers and requests flooded in for his assistance. Before he took up the new challenge, Cardinal de la Torre invited him to address the Eucharistic Congress in Rio de Janeiro. The assembled gathering was impressed by the young Legionary, speaking to them in Spanish and enthusing them with his aura of sanctity. Those Alfie encountered were of the one mind that the young man exuded holiness. While in attendance at the congress, Alfie met up with three other envoys, including Joaquina Lucas, his former Spanish teacher. The four envoys made innumerable contacts with the hierarchies of the universal Church. The demand for their skills was so great that it put pressure on the Legionaries. Alfie saw this as a positive step. Ignoring his delicate health which prevented him from entering religious life in Ireland, he launched himself heart and soul into learning Portuguese in the hope of continuing his work in Brazil.

However, requests came in for Alfie – affectionately christened *el corderito* (the little lamb) – to set up a praesidium in Argentina that had previously refused permission for the Legion to set one up there. The Concilium knew Alfie would do great work in Brazil, but the opportunity to spread the Legion throughout Argentina was an opportunity not to be missed. Besides, the Concilium, knowing Alfie's reputation for winning over hearts and minds, believed he was the key to winning over the continent. They said of him, 'He had only to be sent to a place and its doors would open'. Alfie landed in Argentina in 1955 to begin his work. Within a year he had travelled extensively, meeting with the people and impressing many bishops who granted permission for the Legion to establish branches within their dioceses.

From Argentina, Alfie travelled to the neighbouring countries of Bolivia, Paraguay and further north to Ecuador, often in the company of fellow Legionary, Oonagh Twomey, who did her initial training with Alfie. He was delighted to find that within the inhospitable terrain of Ecuador, branches of the Legion were springing up like mushrooms. This was not so in Buenos Aires, the populous capital that kept its doors shut to the Legion. In 1957, Rome divided the capital into five dioceses. Four dioceses accepted the Legion, with the fifth finally following. Buenos Aires eventually became the hub of Legionary work, establishing over two thousand branches.

Alfie led by example. He went out among the poor and the destitute, encouraging Legionaries to help the prostitutes, and showing young seminarians how to set up Legion branches. He even brought a lapsed Catholic back to the Church through the Legion, who then went on to become a priest. On another occasion, Alfie accompanied a local priest on a hospital visit. The priest informed Alfie that he could do little as the man was a non-Christian. Alfie spent time with the sick man and informed the priest that the man wanted to be baptised.

After six years in South America, inspiring and impressing thousands of religious and laity in ten Latin American countries, Alfie asked for permission from Frank Duff to go to Russia. He began learning Russian and was working on ways to enter the Soviet Union when bad health struck. Alfie was diagnosed with inoperable cancer and died in 1959 at only twenty-six years of age. He was laid to rest in the vault of the Christian Brothers in Buenos Aires.

In death, as in life, Alfie continues to inspire. Every year, thousands of locals and Legion members visit his grave asking for and thanking him for favours received. Thousands of young pilgrims walk many miles to pray to him. In 1980, the cause for his beatification was introduced. To many, however, Alfie is already a saint. He has been credited with laying the foundations for the Legion in almost all of the southern hemisphere. The sickly child prone to fainting fits grew up and touched the hearts of thousands. Within a few short years, he brought many souls to his heavenly Mother by blazing a trail across a continent that continues to benefit from his time there.

Edel Quinn

Legion of Mary Envoy

During his infant daughter's baptismal ceremony, the priest asked Charles Quinn what name they had chosen for her. The priest was a little hard of hearing and thought Charles said Edel instead of Adele. So, in 1907, Edel Quinn was baptised in Castlemagner, Co. Cork, the eldest of Charles and Louise Quinn's five children. The name Edel eventually joined the list of popular Irish girls' names, thanks to Edel making her mark as a Legion of Mary Envoy to Africa.

Even as a young girl, Edel displayed a very strong faith. While many young children enjoyed after-Mass activities, Edel preferred spending as much time as possible in Mass and loved nothing more than attending as many Masses as she could. It was a passion carried into adulthood when her working day followed daily Mass attendance. While deeply religious, Edel's interests and activities included piano, dancing, tennis and golf. Described as a bright student, Edel was sent to a girls' finishing school in England. However, family finances took a tumble when her father, a bank manager, developed a gambling problem and was demoted at the bank.

Edel returned to Ireland to help out and secured a secretarial job with Chagny Tile Works in Nassau Street, Dublin. Her hard work, organisational and negotiating skills would stand to her, when, in a few short years, Africa would beckon. Her abilities and warm nature endeared her to her employer, Pierre Landrin, who proposed marriage. Edel graciously refused, informing Pierre that she intended to enter religious life as a Poor Clare. Pierre admired Edel greatly and was deeply moved by her strong faith. He never forgot the high esteem in which he held Edel and when he eventually married, he called one of his daughters after her.

By the 1930s, Edel believed her goal of joining the Poor Clares was in sight. However, illness struck and Edel was diagnosed with tuberculosis in her early twenties. Her family sent her to a sanatorium where she spent over a year. While convalescing, her source of comfort was the writings of St Thérèse of Lisieux. The words of the Little Flower remained with Edel throughout her short life and proved a tremendous source of comfort and inspiration to her. Due to the expense for her family and her belief that her condition was not improving, Edel returned home, but not to the Poor Clares. Her life's journey was not to be a cloistered nun but a missionary who would be an inspiration to countless thousands in a land some seven thousand miles from her home.

Edel had been a Legion member before her illness and she accompanied them on a pilgrimage to Lourdes in 1934, where she felt at home helping and caring for the sick. Two years later, she and Muriel Wailes brought the Legion to England, opening seven praesidia in North Wales. Edel wanted to stay in England evangelising but Frank Duff, founder of the Legion, had more ambitious plans for her. Quick to recognise her organisational skills, Frank asked her to continue with her work in Africa where the Legion was gaining ground. The suggestion was raised at the Concilium but, due to Edel's poor health, was considered unwise. The strongest objection came from a missionary priest, Fr Magennis, who had recently returned from East Africa, where Frank suggested sending Edel. The priest was horrified at the idea of a sickly girl being sent into a place of danger, diseases and primitive conditions and he made his feelings known. Edel rose to speak and informed Fr Magennis that she was fully aware of the situation and realised she was not going on a picnic. Father Magennis quipped that she would be the picnic. The humorous exchange continued when Frank Duff interjected, saying that given her frail physique, she wouldn't make much of a picnic for anyone. Edel, gracious as ever, felt as though she may have been disrespectful to Fr Magennis and apologised to him. Seeing Edel's sincerity, Fr Magennis blessed her and told her to go in God's name to complete his will.

In 1936, the twenty-nine-year-old set sail for Kenya in East Africa. She informed those seeing her off that she didn't expect to return to her native land. The conditions in Africa were everything she had been brought to believe. She encountered difficult terrain, sickness, disease and language barriers, but the worst for Edel was the segregation among the different ethnic and Indigenous groups. The Catholic populations of Africans, Asians, Europeans and Goans refused to mix. Edel would not give in to this, informing them that as children of God they were all equal. She broke down racial and ethnic barriers and persuaded the various groups to attend the Legion meetings as one body, which, eventually, they did.

One Dutch priest who was driving Edel to a Legion of Mary meeting some miles from his mission was moved by her unshakable belief in Our Lady. They encountered a flooded river obscuring the bridge across. The priest was about to turn back when Edel pleaded with him to go forward, telling him, 'I'm sure Our Lady will protect us'. He found himself unable to resist such faith. Some men nearby located the bridge beneath the water and, on a wing and a prayer, the priest drove across the flooded river. Drying out the plugs on the other side, he managed to start the car and they made it to the Legion meeting on time. Such was the unwavering faith and courage of Edel Quinn. When others doubted, her response was always, 'Why can't we trust Our Lady? Our Lady will see after things'.

Overcoming language barriers, Edel recruited translators to prepare the Tessera, the official Legion prayers, into Swahili and various dialects. She faced down threats and curses from witch doctors, unhappy with the encroachment of this foreign religion. In 1938, the Legion purchased a six-year-old Ford car to help her get around. She referred to it as her Rolls Royce. Her driver knew the territory well but had a fondness for the local beer. On too many occasions he was incapable of driving so Edel took on the job of chauffeuring herself.

Those who knew and worked with Edel during her eight years in Africa never ceased to be amazed by her. She thought little of taking on long, arduous journeys through hostile territory to reach mission stations, helping out wherever she could and recruiting new Legionaries to continue with the work. She established groups of local lay people to teach and spread the Catholic faith. Her tremendous contribution to the Legion of Mary in Africa proved a boon to the overworked missionary nuns and priests. Her religious zeal was curtailed on occasions when she suffered with bouts of malaria, pleurisy and dysentery. Undeterred, Edel struggled on, establishing hundreds of praesidia in Kenya, Uganda and Tanzania. Thanks to her efforts, in Africa alone, thousands of Africans are engaged in the work of evangelisation.

In 1940, she set sail across the Indian Ocean to the island of Mauritius. Within nine months she had established thirty Legion praesidia in nineteen different parishes. On her return to East Africa, word of her death had spread. When one missionary priest realised she was still among the living, he wrote a humorous letter to her informing her he was delighted she was still alive. Edel replied in kind, thanking him for his prayers and the Mass to help her out of Purgatory. Her worry, she light-heartedly informed him, was that when she did die, no one would believe it.

Even with good humour and determination, Edel could not prevent the inevitable. Her declining health worsened. She fought for as long as she could, refusing to give in to tropical diseases and pleurisy and somehow managed to go the extra mile before finally surrendering to death. Her deep faith, constant prayer and private suffering was what kept her close to God. She wrote, 'What a desolation life would be without the Eucharist'.

She died in Nairobi in 1944 in her thirty-seventh year, but her legacy lives on. In 1994, Pope John Paul II declared Edel Quinn Venerable. Her home parish erected a statue to her in the grounds of Castlemagner Church. True to her word, Edel never returned home. She died as she lived, in the service of God. Clutching her crucifix tight, she asked those present, 'Is Jesus coming?' Then she smiled gently, kissed the cross and uttered her last word: 'Jesus.'

LAITY

Venerable Matt Talbot

Dublin's Saint in the Making

No one paid much attention to the twelve-year-old boy making his way to work. No questions were asked as to why he wasn't at school. There was no compulsory school-leaving age at that time, so it was normal for boys this young to be in the workforce. Joining their ranks was Matt Talbot, one of six surviving siblings from a family of twelve children. Matt, whose scant education in O'Connell's Christian Brothers Primary School, was remembered by the Brother who taught him as 'a mitcher' – a reference to his penchant for truancy. When he entered the workforce in 1868 as a messenger boy for the beer-bottling firm E. & J. Burke, Matt could neither read nor write. Born just seven years after Ireland's Great

Hunger, which ended in 1849, education did not play a big part for many of Ireland's poor, struggling families. Matt's mother, Elizabeth, worked as a charwoman, and his father, Charles, worked in the stores of the Port and Docks Board on Custom House Quay.

Matt's entry into the workforce brought an added dimension into his young life that would plague him for several years. Observing his fellow workers helping themselves to the ready supply of alcohol, he soon followed suit. The endless supply of tipples hastened his fondness for alcohol. After four years with his first employer, Matt moved from E. & J. Burke to the Port and Docks Board where his father worked. The new job change didn't put an end to Matt's drinking, it merely introduced him to the hard stuff – whiskey. By the age of sixteen, Matt was often returning home drunk. He continued his working life as an unskilled labourer. The work was hard, and hard work called for hard drinking. Matt was described as a functioning alcoholic, working by day and drinking by night, every night. He often accompanied his two brothers, Philip and Joe, to the local pub.

Most, if not all, of Matt's wages were spent on drink. When he regularly exhausted those, he borrowed and scrounged for drink money. Alcoholism knows no shame and so it was with Matt, who resorted to pawning his clothes and boots and engaging in thievery to buy his next drink. He would later recall to a friend an incident that, in retrospect, he was very much ashamed of. A fiddle player once joined Matt and his friends for a drink, and, unbeknownst to the man, they stole his fiddle and pawned it to buy more alcohol. Years later, Matt made a great effort to find the man to make restitution, but to no avail. To make amends, Matt had Masses said for him.

To supplement his wages in order to feed his alcoholism, Matt would take on extra work. The young man wasn't drinking to live but living to drink. His life was spiralling out of control. Matters came to a head when, in 1884, he and his two brothers found themselves out of work. Standing outside their local pub, the men were sure their drinking pals would stand them a round. It didn't happen. Their friends chose to ignore them and passed them by. Matt took it particularly hard and, later, admitted to feeling deeply hurt, as he had been generous to them when finances allowed. Now snubbed by those he associated with, the disillusioned Matt returned home. At that juncture in his life, and guided by a higher power, he was unknowingly turning his back on his second home and a way of life that had held him prisoner for some fourteen years. Matt Talbot's journey towards sobriety and spiritual awakening was about to begin.

On his return home, Matt informed his mother – who was surprised to see her son home so early – that he was going to take the pledge. She advised him not to take the pledge unless he intended keeping it. Matt's retort was, 'By the grace of God I'll be able to keep it'. He made his way to Clonliffe College Seminary, where a priest persuaded him to try to remain sober for ninety days. To avoid after-work drinking, Matt went for walks and when he felt tired he called into the nearest church to rest. Finding the withdrawal symptoms difficult, Matt told his mother, 'It's no use, mother, I'll drink again when the three months are up'. Later, in an interview, his sister said, 'During the three months, as the religion gripped him, he got fonder and fonder of the church and used to live in it after his work was done'.

During one of his walks, the smell of alcohol emanating from a public house enticed Matt inside. Standing at the crowded bar, he was luckily unobserved by the busy barman. Receiving no service, Matt left the bar and made his way into a Jesuit church. He made himself another promise never to carry money with him, so if he lapsed again, he would not have the funds to buy a drink. It was a promise he kept for the rest of his life.

Having survived his first three months sober, Matt extended the pledge to six months. His daily life soon included attending 5 a.m. Mass before starting his day's work. He was initially helped on his spiritual journey by Fr James Walsh and, later, by Monsignor Michael Hickey, who became a spiritual coach and close friend to Matt. He taught Matt how to read and write, giving him an introduction to early Irish monasticism and Celtic spirituality, which impacted greatly on the recovering alcoholic. His reading life extended to the lives of the saints. When asked how an uneducated man could understand Cardinal Newman's *Apologia,* Matt replied that he always prayed to God for understanding of the material he was reading or at least the main points of the book. Much of Matt's writings, found after his death, were on scraps of paper. They contained quotes from the Bible, the fine points of an interesting sermon, or notes on saintly qualities.

Aping the early monks, Matt rose at 2 a.m. for prayer before attending 5 a.m. Mass. He would return home for an early breakfast of dry bread and a mixture of tea and cocoa before starting his day's work. The main meals of his day were similar to his breakfast. His spartan life had begun. Sleeping quarters for the austere Matt contained a wooden plank for his bed and a wooden pillow to rest his head. He allowed himself a sheet and a thin blanket for comfort and warmth.

Some years after Matt's full conversion, he confided to a friend about his encounter with unseen demonic forces. All too often, saints in the making are blocked from God's path by the diabolical. Matt grappled with an evil force that violently pushed him away from the door of St Francis Xavier Church as he attempted to enter. This unseen hand thwarted Matt's second and third attempt to enter the church. Matt's resilience won out and, on that occasion, the infernal interference stopped and the penitent entered his beloved church. The second attempt was an attack on his mind. Sunday morning Mass was interrupted as he approached the altar to receive the consecrated host. An inner voice told him that his desire to drink would return and all his pious actions were useless. Matt began to despair and found himself physically incapable of approaching the altar. A compulsion caused him to leave the church, where he felt free of the terrible oppression. On entering other churches to receive Communion, the blackness of despair continued to consume him and he was forced to leave. Eventually, arriving back at St Francis Xavier Church, he threw himself prostrate on the steps and cried out, 'Surely, oh Lord, I am not going to fall again into the habits I have left'. Imploring the Blessed Virgin to intercede for him, which She did, Matt was now able to attend 10 a.m. Mass and receive Holy Communion. The struggle to receive Communion lasted some three hours before he, with the help of Our Lady, was able to overcome it. He was never assailed in this way again.

Matt's personal life was one of a celibate lay man. His mother recounted that he refused the offer of marriage to a young cook who proposed to him, after making a novena to Our Lady for guidance. He later informed his friends that marriage would interfere with the religious path he had chosen for himself. His life revolved around hard work and prayer. By 1892, Matt found employment as a labourer in the timber yard of T. & C. Martin. The change from bricklaying suited him best, as the later start in the timber yard coincided with a change in Mass times at St Francis Xavier's Church. The 8 a.m. work start allowed Matt to attend Mass at 6 a.m., before beginning a long, arduous day's work. Through good example and pious behaviour, Matt had a lasting effect on many of his fellow workers, who refrained from using bad language in his presence. Every spare minute he had was used in silent prayer. Leading by example, he often tried to solve disputes between his fellow workers. He encouraged many of them to stay on the path back to God. Remembered by those who knew him as a hard-working man who loved a good joke and funny story – provided no profane language was used – he was generous to families in need and encouraged pious young men to grow in holiness.

In the world, but not quite of the world, Matt didn't involve himself in the turbulent politics of the time. When asked about his views on the civil war that ended in 1923, Matt said he sincerely regretted that Irish men were killing each other. During the 1913 Lockout, he initially refused strike pay, believing he had no right to accept money when he wasn't working to earn it. When asked by a friend what he thought of the strike, he said – after consulting with a Jesuit Father in his church who lent him a book on the matter – that no one had the right to starve the poor into submission. This cleared his conscience on accepting strike pay. He lent most of his working capital to fellow workers who were more in need than himself. Preferring to lend money, he felt it would encourage the borrower to pay it back, rather than spending it in a bar.

Following the death of his father Charles in 1899, who died age seventy-three, Matt went to live with his mother in Upper Rutland Street. Observing her son often in prayer, she informed her daughter that his nightly prayers were offered up kneeling on his hard wooden bed or lying prostrate on the floor. She believed Matt was in ecstasy and often heard him converse with the Blessed Virgin. Matt never spoke about his nightly prayer vigil but his mother truly believed he ascended to a higher spiritual plane during this time. He once confided to a close friend that he had asked for the gift of prayer and had received it in abundance. Speaking to his sister Susan, he complained of the lack of the love of God among men: 'Susan, if I could only tell you of the great joy I had last night talking to God and the Blessed Virgin.' Even his demeanour in the church led one of the Jesuit priests to observe that they had a saint in attendance.

In 1909, Matt was introduced to the writings of St Louis-Marie de Montfort when his friend, Ralph O'Callaghan, gave him a book entitled, *True Devotion to Mary*. The book suggested that a sign of consecration to Jesus, through Mary, was to wear a chain around the body. This was an idea that really appealed to Matt, so much so that with the zeal of the converted, he wore not one chain, but three, for the rest of his life. The man described as 'a saint in overalls' caught the attention of two popes. In 1975, fifty years after Matt's death, Pope St Paul VI declared Matt Venerable, the second stage on the road to sainthood. Matt's life story also impacted on Pope St John Paul II. He was greatly impressed by Matt's devotion to Our Lady and wanted him to be beautified and canonised.

Two years before Matt's death, in 1925, his health went into decline. Living alone since his mother's death in 1915, he was hospitalised with kidney and heart conditions. He fought as long as he could, continuing on his rigorous path to salvation, observing – when his health allowed – his strict fast, daily Communion and continuing to work. The Sunday morning of his death, he trod familiar ground on the way to St Saviour's Dominican Church in Granby Lane. Before reaching the door of the church, he collapsed. He was observed by Mrs Anne Keogh and her son, who ran over to help him. However, Matt had taken his last breath in this world.

In life, Matt Talbot went mostly unnoticed. This was how the man who lived a quiet, saintly life would have wanted it. However, his death wasn't the end – it was the beginning of a lasting legacy that has spread around the world. The chains found around the body of the sixty-nine-year-old caused questions to be asked by those who didn't know him, but for those who did know him, no explanation was necessary. This was how their brother, friend and work colleague had decided to live. Matt Talbot was a hard-working reformed alcoholic, who had chosen a path of suffering and perseverance towards his heavenly reward.

Shortly after his death, a small pamphlet was printed in memoriam of Matt. It grew in momentum and calls were made throughout the universal Church for further details of this remarkable man. Within a short space of time, Matt's fame had reached Australia and his life story, *Life of Matt Talbot, A Dublin Labourer*, was translated into some fourteen different languages. This first written account of Matt's life details numerous favours received by those who prayed to him for help. Matt Talbot is considered the man to pray to for help in overcoming drug and alcohol addiction.

His initial burial place was in a pauper's grave in Glasnevin Cemetery. In 1956, as part of the process for canonisation, his body was exhumed. In 1972, it was finally laid to rest in Our Lady of Lourdes Church, Sean McDermott Street, Dublin. People from around the world come to his shrine asking him for help with addiction and recovery. A statue of Matt stands by the Talbot Memorial Bridge over the River Liffey, near the Dublin docks, and a bronze plaque marks the site of his death. In 2006, Timothy Schmalz, a Canadian sculptor who predominantly focuses on religious figures, donated a bronze plaque to St Mary's Pro Cathedral, Dublin, on the 150th anniversary of Matt's birth and baptism.

The twelve-year-old boy who took his first steps into the world of work and the ravages of alcoholism would later learn to endure and overcome. Matt Talbot's example has been of enormous help to many suffering from addictions. Perhaps his life and legacy could be summed up thus: 'The Kingdom of Heaven was promised not to the sensible and the educated but to such as have the spirit of little children.' An ordinary man who did extraordinary things may give Dublin another saint.

Little Nellie of Holy God

Suffer the Little Children to Come Unto Me

It is not often that a child of four years of age influences the decision of a pope. Yet that is apparently what happened in the case of little Nellie Organ of Holy God. Pope Pius X had been considering allowing children from age seven to receive Holy Communion. He had prayed to God for guidance before making this important decision, and his prayer was answered when he was given a book on the extraordinary life of Ireland's little Nellie. Pope Pius also received a letter from Bishop O'Callaghan of Cork, giving further testimony to this amazing little girl. When the pope read the life of little Nellie, he was so moved by her sanctity that he took this as God's answer and, in August 1910, he promulgated that children from the age of seven could receive Holy Communion.

The spiritually precocious little Nellie received Holy God in December 1907 at the tender age of four, two months before her death in February 1908. Ellen (Nellie) Organ was the youngest child of William Organ – believed to be a derivative of the name Hogan – and Mary Ahern. Nellie had three older siblings – Thomas, David and Mary. Their father was a labouring man and he and his wife brought the children up in the practice of their faith. Little Nellie had a particular love for the family rosary and, following the example of her beloved mother, she would kiss each bead as she prayed. When William was faced with unemployment, he joined the British Army in 1897 and was stationed at the garrison in Waterford. The family remained there for a number of years until his wife Mary contracted tuberculosis. They transferred to the army barracks on Spike Island in Cork Harbour, believing that the air was fresher and better for her health. However, in January 1907, two years after their move, Mary died. The family was devastated. Unable to look after his young children, William placed them into State care. Mary and little Nellie were placed with the Good Shepherd Sisters in Cork.

Both sisters had whooping cough and, before long, little Nellie would be diagnosed with more serious ailments that would see her confined to the orphanage infirmary for the remainder of her short life. It was noted that when Nellie had to sit still for any length of time, she would often burst into tears. Another girl, who slept in the adjoining bed to Nellie, said she would cry throughout the night. Often Nellie was seen walking with her arms held out in front, as though she was fearful of falling. When the child was examined, it was discovered she had curvature of the spine, which accounted for the pain and discomfort. The customary industrial boots she wore were considered too heavy for her frail limbs, so the Sisters had lightweight shoes and pretty pink socks made for her.

From her early days in the orphanage, Nellie endeared herself to many. She was generous – when she was given a treat, she would usually offer half to the giver. She was also strong-willed. On one occasion, the breakfast milk was burnt and little Nellie was not pleased. She made her way, mug and spoon in hand, to the presiding Sister. Putting her spoon in the burnt milk she said, 'Mother, taste that'.

One day in the school yard, Nellie ignored the bell summoning the children for supper and remained playing outside. The Sister told her she must not be naughty and keep the children late for supper. Nellie replied:

'They could go if they wanted. They did go and leave me alone.'

Sister asked, 'Are you sorry?'

'Yes I am sorry,' replied Nellie.

'Then tell God you are,' said Sister.

Instantly, Nellie went on her knees. 'Holy God I am very sorry for keeping the girls late for supper. Please forgive me and make me a good child and bless me and my mother.'

It was believed that Nellie had conversations with Holy God while she was on Spike Island, but those around her put it down to childish imagination. Her conversations with Holy God would become more pronounced and led the religious to consider if they had, in their midst, a little saint in the making.

One day while in school, Nellie swallowed some beads she had been playing with. She was taken to the doctor who extracted the beads and gave Nellie a thorough examination. His finding devastated her carer, Nurse Hall, and the Sisters. Little Nellie had tuberculosis and wasn't going to recover. She was removed to the recovery hospital, where she would remain. Nellie asked for Sister Immaculata and Mother Superior to visit her, which they did. She clung on tight to Sister Immaculata, grasping her crucifix as though she wouldn't let go. The nuns were very moved by her devotion to the crucified Christ, which would deepen in the heart and soul of this little child.

While in the infirmary, Nellie grew closer to Nurse Hall, who was a recent convert to Catholicism. Nellie told Nurse Hall that Holy God had taken her mother and she asked her to be her new mother. Nellie often asked her 'Mother' questions on the faith to which Nurse Hall had to refer to the Sisters for answers. While on Spike Island, Nellie would have been familiar with the term 'lock-up', which was a reference to a prison cell. When Nellie became aware of Holy God in the tabernacle, she referred to Him as being in the lock-up. 'Why am Holy God shut up in that little house?' she enquired of Nurse Hall. 'Mother' explained as best she could, which made Nellie thankful that God was not squeezed into a tight space. Nurse Hall brought Nellie to see the Stations of the Cross. When they stopped at the crucifixion, Nelly asked, 'Why did Him let them hurt Him? Him could stop them.' Nurse explained that Christ died for our sins. The little child cried with deep remorse. Seeming to possess understanding beyond her years, Nellie kept repeating, 'Poor Holy God. Poor Holy God'.

During Nellie's first visit to the Exposition of the Blessed Sacrament, Nurse Hall reported a transformation in the child's countenance and demeanour. In hushed awe, little Nellie pointed to the monstrance, 'Mother. There He is. There is Holy God now'. The encounter lit within the heart and soul of this little child a spiritual flame that burnt with such intense longing that only the reception of Christ in His mystical body could quench it. Nellie, with her delicate little frame, walked between two worlds. Whether she encountered Christ in His mystical body, or saw Him represented in iconic imagery, the results were always the same. Nellie was able to speak to Holy God just as easily as she spoke to 'Mother' or the religious Sisters. When she was shown a statue of the Child of Prague, Nellie was intrigued to discover that this was Holy God as a child. As one child to another, Nellie played with the Christ child and laughed when He danced for her. She also prayed to Him and noticed that she often felt better afterwards. This strengthened her belief in the power of prayer, which she put to good use when Nurse Hall was ill. Nellie asked for the statue to be brought to the infirmary that she shared with nurse. After praying to the Child, Nurse Hall got better, much to the delight of little Nellie. On another occasion, one of the Sisters told her not to be talking to the statue so much. Nellie said that the Child was dancing for her.

The Sister, in her own prayers, asked God that if Nellie was indeed in communion with Him, she would receive a sign. She also asked for money to pay for food for the school. A few days later the convent received a donation. The Sister never doubted again.

On another occasion, Nellie was overheard by Nurse Hall asking the Christ child, who was holding a globe in His hands, if He would let her play with the 'ball' she would give Him her dainty shoes. Nurse Hall light-heartedly reminded her that that wasn't possible. With unshakable conviction, Nellie informed her, 'Oh Him can do that if He pleases'.

As the little child grew deeper in her understanding of Christ, her physical pain intensified. Her jawbone was crumbling as a result of tuberculosis and often her mouth had to be disinfected. Painful as it was, little Nellie clung tight to her crucifix. If they sympathised with her, she would smile and remark, 'What is it compared with what He suffered on the cross for me?' The child also had an uncanny ability to know who had received Holy Communion. One of the girls left in charge of Nellie decided to skip daily Mass and hide out in the kitchen so she could discretely keep an eye on Nellie. After Mass ended, she went in to visit her little charge. 'You did not get Holy God today. I will tell Mother on you,' scolded little

Nellie. The astonished girl decided to test Nellie, believing she had heard her moving about in the kitchen. The next day she repeated her actions, remaining deadly quiet in the kitchen. After Mass time, she went in to see Nellie. The little child fixed her with an intense stare, 'You did not get Holy God today'. The girl asked her how she knew. The child replied, 'No matter. You didn't get Holy God'.

On another occasion, the same girl who was left to look after Nellie while Nurse Hall was elsewhere saw Nellie heading back to her cot, clutching a flower tightly. The girl scolded Nellie for leaving her cot and taking a flower from the small altar in her room. Nellie reminded her that the altar was hers. The girl told her she would inform Nurse Hall on her return, which she did. Nellie told the nurse, 'Him give me the flower. Him did, mother'. Nellie loved God's flowers and insisted that only fresh flowers be left on his altar or in front of His statue. When she became too ill to leave her bed, she often asked Reverend Mother 'if dem dirty flowers were taken away from Holy God'.

During a particularly difficult night, Sister Immaculata visited little Nellie. Nurse Hall asked,

'How are you today, darling? I thought you would have been with Holy God by this time.'

'Oh no,' said Nellie. 'Holy God said I'm not good enough to go yet.'

'What do you know about Holy God?' asked Nurse Hall.

'Him did come and stand there,' said Nellie pointing to the side of the cot. 'And Him did say that.'

Nurse Hall and Sister Immaculata looked at each other in amazement.

'Where is He now?' asked Nurse Hall.

'Him there,' replied Nellie, pointing to the same side of the cot.

'And what was he like?' asked Sister.

'Like that,' replied Nellie, crossing her hands on her breast.

The Sister and nurse were astounded by the little girl's answer. They questioned whether it was a child's vivid imagination or if God had chosen this little soul for a purpose, as He did other little children.

When Reverend Mother visited Nellie, she asked, 'Do you want me to talk to you, baby, or say the rosary?'

'Say the rosary, Mother,' Nellie replied without hesitation.

Mother obliged and a few Hail Marys in, Nellie whispered, 'On your knees, Mother'.

Mother remained sitting and Nellie, with a voice of authority, repeated loudly, 'On your knees, Mother'.

Mother obeyed and later informed the Sisters, with good humour, that she finished her rosary on her knees.

Little Nellie's prayer life was one of attachment to the sufferings of Christ. She often prayed for others and knew who would be healed and who would not. She recited the rosary daily and lovingly kissed each bead. Her crucifix was constantly at her side and when her suffering became unbearable, she would look at the crucifix and say, 'Poor Holy God'. Given Nellie's propensity for prayer and deep understanding of faith matters, the Sisters considered having her confirmed. In October 1907, much to the delight of the convent, Bishop O'Callaghan said he would administer the Sacrament of Confirmation to little Nellie. Nellie, confirmed 'a soldier of Christ', was overjoyed by it all, as she knew it drew her closer to Holy God. She told Nurse Hall, 'I am now Holy God's little soldier. I want Holy God'. This was Nellie's first step towards receiving Communion. She possessed an uncanny ability to know, from her small room, when the Blessed Sacrament was exposed in the chapel. She would request, 'Take me to Holy God. He's not in his lock-up'. Often Nurse Hall worried about leaving her frail little charge to go to Mass. Nellie would insist, 'Mother, go down to get Holy God. Then come back to kiss me'.

Reverend Mother visited little Nellie every evening. One evening Nellie asked, 'Mother when you get Holy God, will you bring Him up to me?' Reverend Mother agreed. Early the next day, Nellie woke Nurse Hall and, with great excitement, asked her to clean the house, as Holy God was coming to visit. When Reverend Mother arrived without Holy God, Nellie wept bitterly and passed the rest of the day in almost total silence. Later that evening she said to Nurse Hall, 'Mother, I did think I would have Holy God today.' This desire to receive Holy God remained with the child. The Sisters were firmly convinced that the little child should be considered mature enough to receive Holy Communion.

Nellie was interviewed by Fr Bury, a Jesuit, who, after speaking with her, was convinced that the child was in full command of her mental faculties and deeply understood what it meant to receive Holy God.

'What is Communion?' asked the Jesuit.

'It is Holy God. It is He who makes the nuns and everyone else holy,' replied Nellie.

The Jesuit approached Bishop O'Callaghan, who agreed to grant her Holy Communion. Nellie was overjoyed. 'I will have Holy God in my heart,' she replied. Neither she nor Nurse Hall got a wink of sleep that night, as Nellie was awake all night asking 'Mother' was it time yet to receive Holy God. Nellie's heart's desire was satisfied and, at the young age of four, she was allowed to receive Holy God. The child's countenance radiated sanctifying grace and the terrible odour from her jawbone was no more. She would often ask to be left alone after receiving Holy Communion so she could go into deep spiritual prayer with Holy God. When asked did she not feel lonely or frightened, she replied,

'Oh no. I was talking to Holy God.'

'What does Holy God say?' asked Sister.

'Holy God said I must not speak of these things,' replied the child.

After her conversations with Holy God, Nellie's appearance changed from a sickly child to one in the full bloom of health. Her eyes became so bright that onlookers knew she was looking into another world, and the aroma around her little bed was one of incense.

Thinking the child had fallen asleep, one of the nuns told Nurse Hall that she would go straight to Heaven as she was without sin. Little Nellie opened her eyes and told the nun that she had sinned as she told a lie once. One day before the end of her short life, Nellie saw Reverend Mother crying. 'Why are you crying, Mother? Don't you know I'm going to Holy God?' Nellie was gifted with insight. She told the Sisters that she would die on the Lord's Day, Sunday, which she did. She asked to be allowed to wear her white Communion dress, as she was going to meet Holy God. Nellie asked to die in the arms of her 'Mother', Nurse Hall, and she asked that she also wear a white dress for God's arrival. Her suffering worsened towards the end. On the hour of her death, the child's eyes fixated on the end of her bed and her eyes filled with tears. Her lips moved as if she was in conversation and her eyes followed movement that only she could see. She looked up at something above her head and the eyes of little Nellie of Holy God finally closed on this world for the last time. She died on 2 February 1908, aged four years and five months.

Little Nellie was laid to rest in St Joseph's Cemetery. Those who accompanied her on her final earthly journey were her sister Mary, Nurse Hall and some of the pupils and nuns with whom she spent her last days. Her grave quickly became a shrine, as word of this remarkable little girl spread. Many visitors to Nellie's grave reported a great sense of calm following their visit. Just over a year after her burial, the Sisters wanted her coffin placed in the grounds of the convent cemetery. They opened the grave in the presence of Nurse Hall, a well-known priest and two reliable witnesses. The little child's body was incorrupt except for a small cavity in the right jaw where the jawbone had been destroyed. Her hair had grown slightly and her little fingers were quite flexible. Her Communion dress and veil had not decayed and her silver medal shone bright.

Reported cases of healings attributed to little Nellie are being investigated. On 8 December 1984, a plaque reading 'The Little Violet of the Holy Eucharist' was erected on the exterior wall of the parish church in Portlaw, Co. Waterford. To honour the little child, crowds of parishioners and people from neighbouring counties were present at the ceremony, presided over by His Lordship, Bishop Russell. Little Nellie's room is preserved on Spike Island, complete with the original tabernacle from which she received Holy God. Visitors can take a glimpse into the past of a child who had a deep understanding of faith and love for Holy God, which seems to be the preserve of saints.

One source claims that little Nellie's siblings, Thomas, David and Mary, went to England after completing their education. One boy joined the Merchant Navy, and the other, like his father, joined the British Army. Mary became a seamstress and sewed for the boys in the Jesuit College in England. Her marriage to a Mr Evans produced two girls and a boy. Mary, we are told, lived into her eighties.

Perhaps little Nellie can assist her followers in their endeavours to have her raised to sainthood. If she could influence Pope St Pius X, then perhaps she can do the same, from Heaven, with Pope Francis.

Dorothy Day

From Sinner to Saint

Dorothy Day is considered to be one of the most remarkable American women and social reformers of the twentieth century. Embracing Catholicism in her thirties, calls have now been made for her canonisation by the diocese of her native New York and vigorously supported by Cardinal Timothy Dolan.

Dorothy did not start out in life with a religious calling to bring about her much-desired social reform. Her early political path as a young student saw her gravitate towards left-wing politics. In 1916, at the age of nineteen, she dropped out of college to channel her talents into writing for the Marxist press, covering topics such as rent strikes, birth control and the peace movement. A year later, she marched defiantly with her sister suffragettes in front of the White House in a women's rights demonstration that resulted in one of many arrests for the young radical. Although she advocated for women's suffrage, she herself refused to vote, preferring anarchy to bureaucracy.

Her bohemian lifestyle in Greenwich Village, New York, didn't lend itself to Catholic moral teaching. An early life fraternising with actors, literary figures and revolutionaries led her into a string of unhappy relationships, an abortion, attempted suicide and a common-law marriage to Forster Batterham that resulted in the birth of her daughter, Tamara.

All during her turbulent early years, Dorothy never lost her strong sense of social injustice, and an overriding desire to help the less fortunate remained with her. This yearning to help the marginalised had been her raison d'être from an early age, helping to form the person she would become.

In 1904, when Dorothy was seven, her father John Day, a Tennessee native of Irish-Scottish stock, took a sportswriter's job in San Francisco. Two years later, the great earthquake of San Francisco left some three thousand dead and almost one quarter of a million homeless. The efforts of the relief workers, including her mother, to help the victims of the quake greatly impressed itself upon Dorothy's young mind and remained with her throughout her life.

During her childhood years, Dorothy, in her own words, found God while reading aloud to her sister from a Bible she found in a house in which they were staying. As she read, she became cognisant of a personality impressing itself upon her and she knew instinctively that it was God. Although Dorothy was baptised into her mother's Episcopalian faith at the age of twelve, she followed in her family's footsteps by seldom attending church. The God that Dorothy discovered as a child was kept at arm's length.

During her wild student days, Dorothy fervently believed that God had died and the new saviours of mankind were to be found in the Communist movement. While she tried to live the life of an agnostic, she could never quite remove the feeling that God was calling her and only He could fill the void in her life.

During her time in Greenwich Village, she often found herself visiting St Joseph's Catholic Church. While not being aware of what was happening on the altar, she took comfort from kneeling at the back of the Church, enjoying the silence and the atmosphere of people in worship.

When her daughter Tamara was born in 1927, Dorothy resolved to have her baptised in the Catholic

Church. For Dorothy, this was the Church of immigrants and the poor, and one that greatly appealed to her. This definitive move towards Catholicism caused the breakup of her union with Forster Batterham, a committed anarchist and atheist who considered their relationship to be a mere comradeship. However, this didn't prevent Dorothy from five years of correspondence with Forster in an attempt to persuade him to marry her and accept her entry into the Catholic Church. It would appear, however, that the only time Forster ever entered the church was to attend a memorial Mass for Dorothy in St Patrick's Cathedral, following her death in 1980. Dorothy's letters revealed her deep desire to spend her Catholic life married to Forster. His refusal to cooperate resulted in Dorothy sacrificing her love for this man for her love of God and His Church.

Dorothy's hunger for helping the poor never subsided and, at times, she found herself frustrated that the wheels of Church bureaucracy seemed to move too slowly. While in prayer, Dorothy asked Christ to show her what she could do to help. Her prayers were answered when she was introduced to Peter Maurin, a French peasant farmer. Maurin taught for a while in Christian Brothers' schools and, following the example of St Francis, lived a life of voluntary poverty. He shared his knowledge of Catholic

Social Teaching with Dorothy and encouraged her to use her journalistic skills to spread this message through the publication of *The Catholic Worker*.

The newspaper first made its appearance on 1 May 1933, when two thousand five hundred copies went on sale on the streets at a cost of one penny. The aim of the paper was to help combat Communism, which many saw as the solution to the Great Depression that was ravishing America. Day and Maurin hoped to inform the Catholic and non-Catholic poor that the solution did not lie with Communism, but with the progressive social teachings of the Catholic Church. The paper went on to inform that it was possible to protest and demand change without needing to eradicate religion, and radicals did not need to become atheists. Within three years, the paper circulation reached one hundred and fifty thousand copies. It continues circulating today and still sells for one penny.

The paper was just the first step in Day and Maurin's quest to feed and house the hungry and the homeless. Bringing Maurin's vision to life, they went on to establish houses of hospitality, as opposed to workhouses, for the poor. The Catholic Worker Movement, as it became known, opened its first two houses in Manhattan in 1933. Today, they number well over one hundred, stretching from the continent of North America, Canada, Europe and encompassing Ireland and the Antipodes.

Dorothy Day has received praise and ridicule in equal measure. Her strong stance on pacifism lost her the support of many of her fellow workers and supporters when she opposed both sides in the Spanish Civil War and disagreed with America's involvement in World War II. Her belief 'love your enemy' was seen as anti-American and sales of her paper drastically declined. However, undeterred, she and Maurin struggled on. Where there was war and conflict, Dorothy opposed it. She never paid taxes, refused to salute the flag and, on occasions, compared some Catholic prelates to sharks.

The Catholic rebel with a cause followed in Christ's footsteps by living with the poor and marginalised and by spending some fifty years of her life putting the Gospel message into effect.

In 1996, Dorothy's life was brought to the big screen by Fr Bud Kieser, known as the showbusiness priest. The movie *Entertaining Angels* told Dorothy's story, warts and all. Playing the role of Peter Maurin, Martin Sheen spoke of giving something back to the Catholic Worker Movement. Sheen vividly recalled his days as a struggling actor in 1959 New York, when the Catholic houses fed him body and soul.

Dorothy Day has been described by Fr Kieser as Mother Teresa with a past. Dorothy met Mother Teresa on two separate occasions, once in Calcutta. Both women had a genuine love of the poor and a deep Catholic conviction. Dorothy Day was a daily communicant, a devotee of the rosary and a grandmother of nine. Her path from sinner to saint was not in vain. She has been an inspiration to many and even received greetings on her eightieth birthday from Pope Paul VI.

Father Kieser believes Dorothy has earned her sainthood. After all, he explained, she surrendered her life to God and gave Him a chance to work through her. That, he said, is what makes a saint.

Whether or not Dorothy will be canonised remains in the hands of the Church hierarchy. She never considered herself saintly but believed in what St Paul had to say – that everyone was called to sainthood. For many, it would appear that Dorothy Day, Catholic radical, pacifist and social reformer, certainly answered that call.

Élisabeth Leseur

The Good Wife

In 1889, a genteel Parisian lady named Élisabeth Arrighi married the love of her life, Felix Leseur. During the early years of their marriage, Élisabeth's thoughts were far from the profound. The childless couple enjoyed all that upper-class Parisian society had to offer – expensive restaurants, nightly entertainment and socialising with the bourgeoisie.

Although both husband and wife were from respectable Catholic families, as a young medical student, Felix lost his faith while studying in Paris. He kept quiet about this as he did not wish to upset his parents and, when he married Élisabeth, he promised himself that he would not interfere with her Catholicism. This was a promise he was to break.

Felix's journey into spiritual darkness found an outlet in the Parisian anti-clerical newspapers. He wrote articles for the papers and eventually became editor of *Century*. As his radical atheism progressed, so too did his dislike of his wife's nominal Catholicism. He became frustrated with what he saw as an intelligent, cultured woman believing in such superstition and was determined to free her from her foolish notions. He later admitted that he sought out ammunition to argue against Catholicism and set himself the task of attacking Élisabeth's faith in order to deprive her of it. He said, 'May God pardon me. I nearly succeeded'.

In his quest to prove there was no God, Felix built up an impressive library of anti-Catholic books based on freethinking, modernism and liberal Protestantism. He was so emphatic about Élisabeth sharing in his reading tastes that she began to find stimulus from these anti-Catholic ideas. Felix was delighted by this and felt she was ready at last to receive the truth. He presented her with his pièce de resistance, Ernest Renan's book, *The Life of Jesus,* which questioned the divinity of Christ. While Élisabeth embraced the book, she found it shallow and lacking substance, much to the annoyance of her husband who redoubled his efforts to convert her.

Élisabeth's brush with anti-Catholicism set her on an unexpected course. Her curiosity aroused, she determined to understand more about her childhood religion. She studied the Gospels, read the Fathers of the Church and the Lives of the Saints, and applied her intelligence to the study of Philosophy and Modern Languages. Élisabeth was more than a match for Felix and his intellectual circle of friends who frequently visited the Leseur household to discuss the values of atheism and the irrationality of Catholic belief. Élisabeth wrote in her many journals of her distress of listening to her husband and friends verbally attack her religion and her love of the Risen Christ. However, she took it all in her stride, determined not to allow this to weaken her love for her Felix or disrupt the harmony of their married life.

Love between Felix and Élisabeth was never an issue. It was Felix's slide into anti-Catholicism that caused Élisabeth so much worry. She wrote in her journal that she would not be able to fully enjoy the beauty and happiness of Heaven knowing that her beloved Felix had put himself beyond salvation. As Élisabeth entered more fully into Catholic mysticism, she came to appreciate the value of suffering. In 1905, she recorded in her journal that she had asked Almighty God to send her sufficient sufferings to purchase the soul of her husband. She then recorded, 'On the day that I die, the price will have been paid'. Élisabeth got her request. She suffered terribly from chronic liver disease and breast cancer. However, this did not deter her from working with families less fortunate than herself. No matter how ill she felt, she greeted those who came to see her with a smile and a word of encouragement.

In 1910, the Leseurs went on a trip to the Hôtel-Dieu, a hospice run by nursing Sisters. During the first of only two visits, Élisabeth met Sr Marie Goby, who would become her spiritual soulmate. Through correspondences, Élisabeth confided her innermost thoughts to Sr Goby and spoke of her sufferings for Felix's conversion. The good Sister understood the value of prayer and suffering, and also prayed for Felix to return to his faith.

In 1912, Élisabeth made a trip to Lourdes. While there, Felix witnessed a sight that defied belief, though it was not enough at the time to dispel his disbelief in anything miraculous. As a doctor and atheist, he felt it criminal to offer the sick and dying false hope, but he had to concede that something was giving great joy and peace to the afflicted. It was when he saw his wife in prayer before the statue of the Blessed Virgin that he realised the supernatural was at work. Élisabeth appeared to levitate. Felix later wrote that the spectacle disturbed him, but on his return to Paris it faded, at least on the surface, from his mind. At that time in his life it was not a sufficient deterrent from debunking Lourdes in a book he planned to write.

By 1913, Élisabeth's cancer had spread. She turned fervently to prayer only to be mocked by Felix who considered prayer childish. However, in later writings he admitted that his wife's radiance touched him deeply and he knew this was the radiance of a soul belonging entirely to God. Even visitors to the Leseur household spoke of a similar experience. One friend advised his wife that whenever she was anxious, she should visit Élisabeth and bathe in her serenity.

Élisabeth died in 1914, aged forty-seven. The countless mourners at her funeral expressed such genuine grief that the clergy wanted to know who she was as they had never witnessed such a funeral. Before Élisabeth passed away, she spoke prophetic words to Felix: 'I shall die before you. And when I am dead, you will be converted; and when you are converted, you will become a religious. You will be Fr Leseur.'

Felix felt his world collapse after Élisabeth's death, but he balked at the suggestion that he would enter religious life. He considered Élisabeth's words to be nothing more than the fanciful notions of a pious woman. However, going through her journal, he discovered another dimension to his beloved wife. He realised that she had made a pact with God. She offered her life for his salvation. Her death and journal touched him so deeply that it began a revolution in his soul which led to his spiritual journey home. Felix wrote: 'When I think that I was foolish enough to try to destroy the Faith that lifted her so high and sustained her so powerfully! To what a hell would I have reduced her and condemned myself at the same stroke.' With his wife still guiding him, Felix answered the call and made his confession. Not only was he reconciled to the Church he had attempted to destroy, he also felt a call to enter religious life.

Such was his anti-clerical reputation, that when he met Pope Benedict XV to discuss entering religious life, the pope refused and instructed him to remain in the world and repair the damage he had done to the Church. However, the pope recanted and, in 1923, Felix became a Dominican priest. To give something back to his beloved wife, he published her journal, which started the cause for her beatification. For Élisabeth Leseur, her spiritual battle was won. Her beloved husband, Fr Felix Leseur, died in 1950. Élisabeth's victory was complete.

José Sánchez del Río

Little Saint of the Revolution

José Sánchez del Río was born in 1913, three years after the start of the Mexican Revolution. The political machinations of ambitious men vying for power meant little to the young boy at first. He would be in his fourteenth year before the revolution would impact upon him, taking his life in the most brutal fashion. The boy's courage in the face of death and his undying love for Christ and the Virgin of Guadeloupe resounded within and outside of Mexico. The story of José refused to die and his faith led to his canonisation by Pope Francis in October 2016.

José was one of many martyrs during this repressive period when the Mexican Government, under the leadership of President Plutarco Elías Calles, elected in 1924, determined to destroy the Catholicism of the Mexican people. Boasting to the French ambassador, Calles informed him that once the people were denied Mass and the sacraments, they would soon forget their faith and the war, waged by Mexican Catholics, would soon be over. Following the Jacobin agenda of the French Revolution of 1789, President Calles sought the complete destruction of the Catholic Church. The president wanted to centralise power in the hands of the federal government and considered the Church an obstacle to his ambitions. He enforced Articles contained in the 1917 Constitution that curtailed religious practices. These restrictions became known as Calles Law. By 1926, the Catholic Church was forced to go underground. Foreign priests were exiled, Church property seized by the government, priests and religious murdered and churches desecrated. The way of life for the people became unbearable and many of them joined the ranks of the Cristeros soldiers who rose up to defend Christ the King and venerate Our Lady of Guadalupe.

Witnessing the persecution of his people and his Church, the young José wanted to join his two older brothers in the ranks of the Cristeros. Reluctantly, his parents gave their permission, hoping that he would not be involved in the fighting. Before he left his family for the last time, he informed them, 'For Jesus Christ, I will do everything'. This was a promise he did not break. Reaching a Cristeros camp, José and his young friend were given menial chores. José attended Mass regularly and prayed the rosary with the soldiers. He was taught to play the bugle for battle and fell under the care of General Luis Morfin. It is believed that, hoping to protect the boy, the general gave him the duty of standard bearer. During a skirmish in 1928, the general's horse was killed. José offered the general his own horse but refused to ride with him, believing it would slow the general down. The general pleaded with the boy to ride with him but José informed him that a general was more important to the war than a boy. José's parting words to the general were, 'Viva Cristo Rey!', meaning 'Long Live Christ the King'. José remained behind on the field of battle and was eventually captured by the federalist troops. He was asked by a federal officer to switch sides, but he declined to do so. His refusal sealed his fate.

José's defiance and that of his fellow Catholics against the 'Jacobin agenda', were brought to the attention of the White House by the Catholic hierarchy and the Knights of Columbas. The Knights had members in Mexico since 1905 and their organisation came under persecution from the Mexican Government. The organisation spent one million dollars informing the American people of the persecutions and the atrocities taking place just over the border. The Knights lobbied President Calvin Coolidge, seeking his help to end the violence. They mobilised American Catholics and their actions resulted in a backlash from the then powerful Ku Klux Klan, who supported and financed President Calles. The Knights lost several of their members, martyred at the hands of the Mexican Government, including six priests declared saints in 2000 by Pope John Paul II. The pressure brought to bear on the Calles government eventually helped pave the way to an uneasy peace. The Cristeros army laid down their arms in 1929, ending their three-year war. However, they were unhappy with the outcome. While religious restrictions were somewhat eased, they were not removed from the statute books. It meant that future governments could reintroduce Calles Laws if they so wished. Relations between Church and State were tense for years to follow, with atheistic Communism attempting to control the educational system of Mexico's Catholic children.

After 'peace' was declared, President Calles ordered the executions of some five hundred Cristero leaders and five thousand men were also shot, often in front of their wives and children. Their property was seized, ensuring destitution for their families. It has been claimed that the presidency of Plutarco Calles witnessed the bloodiest years in Mexico's history. During the Cristero War, some one hundred thousand people died on both sides. Among them was young José Sánchez del Río. One of his last letters to his mother, written from his prison cell in February 1928, saw the boy resign himself to his fate. He told his mother he would die happy as he was on the side of God. José was imprisoned in the church where he had been baptised. The federal troops turned the church into a stable and desecrated the once-beautiful building beyond recognition.

News of José's arrest spread rapidly. Attempts were made to secure his release, but to no avail. His godfather, Rafael Picazo, a local dignitary who was sympathetic to Calles's administration, attempted to destroy the boy's loyalty to the Cristeros by encouraging him to join forces with the Federal Army. José informed his godfather that he would rather die than join forces with the persecutors of the Church. He replied loudly, 'Viva Cristo Rey! Viva La Virgen de Guadalupe!' His godfather handed him over to his executioners. The boy secretly received Holy Communion for the last time before his torturous death. The federal guards beat the boy and cut the soles of his feet – some reports claim his feet were skinned – before making him walk to his death. He was repeatedly stabbed before being shot. He is reported to have proclaimed with his dying breath, 'Viva Cristo Rey!'

News quickly spread of the boy martyr and people began praying to him. In 2005, José was beatified by Pope Benedict XVI. His canonisation followed when the Vatican approved a miracle attributed to him that saved the life of a baby suffering from incurable brain damage. The little saint of the revolution gave the Catholic Church another martyr. 'Viva Cristo Rey!'

Enrique Ernesto Shaw

God's Businessman

In Mark's Gospel we are told, 'It is easier for a camel to pass through the eye of a needle than for a rich man to enter the Kingdom of God'. These words could never be said to apply to Argentinian businessman, Enrique Ernesto Shaw. Born in France in 1921 to Argentinian parents, the unassuming family man and father of nine broke the mould. Living his Catholic faith to the full, the businessman embraced Catholic Social Teaching in his working life and brought his children up in the fullness of their faith.

Enrique's mother Sara died in 1925, just two years after the family returned to Argentina from France. Enrique was only four years of age. He and his brother were reared by their father, Alejandro, and their aunts. Their father, a non-practising Catholic, kept his promise to his dying wife to have the children instructed in the Catholic faith. Alejandro was founder and president of Shaw Bank in Argentina and the children enjoyed the benefits of a financially secure and happy upbringing. However, it was a young family without a mother – a loss keenly felt by all children. Enrique drew close to the Blessed Virgin and kept her as an integral part of his life, often approaching her in his prayers for guidance. He was an outstanding student at the De La Salle School in Buenos Aires and was noted for his academic abilities. Serving as an altar boy, he became a daily communicant and he maintained his religious observance throughout his adult life.

In 1936, at the tender age of fifteen, Enrique joined the Argentine Navy. One of its youngest recruits, Enrique endured the taunts of his fellow sailors who often chided him for his religious leanings and teased him when he knelt to say his nightly prayers. The young man bore it well and, like a true evangelist, he took every opportunity to explain Catholic teaching, encouraging the sailors to attend Mass and receive Holy Communion. Through his own good example, he won the respect of his fellow sailors. One mother wrote to Enrique thanking him for bringing her son back to the Church. Every path in Enrique's life was an opportunity to spread the Gospel message and proselytise those whom he encountered. His diary entries were between himself and God, outlining his thoughts on how best he could serve his heavenly Father. Enrique firmly believed that God allowed him to know his sins so that he could correct his faults and failings, bringing him closer to God and enabling him to serve Him best.

Enrique remained in naval service, making his way to officer status. In 1943, at the age of twenty-two, his thoughts turned to marrying a young lady he had known for years. Similar to Enrique, the twenty-two-year-old Cecilia Bunge came from a wealthy background. She too lost her mother when she was young. Both fathers approved of the union as it brought together two prominent and prestigious families. However, all that was lost on Enrique, who merely saw it as a marriage of love between himself and his beautiful bride. Cecilia remembered the day of the engagement party which was missing the intended bridegroom. She received a letter from Enrique informing her that he would not be able to make it to the party. Following a disagreement with the admiral, he was sent to prison for three days, but, with good humour, he told Cecilia to continue with the party in his absence. He did, however, make it home in time for his wedding.

In 1945, two years after his wedding, the navy sent Enrique to Illinois in Chicago to study meteorology. His life in the navy was taking him away from his family. When he could not be present for the birth of his first son, Enrique felt the need to leave the navy. It was a desire that would not only keep him close to his family, it would also enable him to continue as a lay missionary, spreading the Gospel to a new audience.

When Cecilia's uncle offered him a senior position in Cristalerias Rigolleau glass factory, he was reluctant to accept. He felt he could do more good working alongside the men on the factory floor. Enrique believed he would understand the problems of those less well-off and be in a better position to help them financially and to reach them with the Gospel message. He was encouraged to remain at top management where it was felt he could do even more good for the workers. As a senior manager, he broke down barriers between the factory floor staff and management. He listened to union delegates in order to learn about and resolve worker grievances. The workforce soon came to realise that Enrique was a very different kind of boss – one they could relate to. If he knew an employee had a problem at home or at work but did not go to him, Enrique sought them out and did his utmost to help them.

When he travelled to different places in Europe, including the Vatican, it enabled him to observe the world of worker and entrepreneur. He wanted to improve his knowledge so he could benefit his employees and make the factory a more friendly place where they felt valued. Employees remembered him with great fondness. Stories abound of his generosity towards the workers. Whenever he was planning a business trip, he would take a list of requests from employees for items they could not get in Argentina. Cecilia remembered a particular trip they made to America. One employee requested a particular cigarette lighter that was only available in America. Cecilia almost wore out her shoe leather trying to find the lighter. When she informed Enrique that she could not find it, he encouraged her to keep looking and buy something similar. He reminded her how fortunate they were, being able to travel to different countries, compared to the workforce who could never afford to leave Argentina.

As managing director, Enrique paid out yearly bonuses. If he knew an employee was saving to build a house, he put extra money into the bonus. When one of the men asked about the extra money he had received, not realising Enrique knew he was saving for a house, Enrique happily replied that it would buy an extra window for his house.

In 1952, Enrique and his fellow business associates founded the Christian Association of Business Executives (ACDE), with Enrique being appointed president of the organisation. The august body was seen as the answer for those who wanted a Catholic Argentina. The entrepreneurs were encouraged to bring Catholic Social Teaching into the workplace. Their skills were the lifeblood of the country and they were encouraged to work not solely for their own financial reward but for the greater good of society. Enrique was to the forefront of bringing in a new law that benefitted families. He also established a pension fund, health care plan, medical services and financial support in times of illness and after the birth of a child.

Sara Shaw, one of Enrique's daughters, remembered him always coming home from work in great form. His playful nature turned their family life into one of great joy. He often turned down after-work activities with colleagues, preferring instead to spend his free time with his children. He left his work problems at the front door. The family prayed the daily rosary. Enrique was a great believer in the adage, 'the family that prays together, stays together'. Cecilia spoke of his love for each of his nine children. When one of their sons was eight, he had serious health problems that required several operations. Enrique spoke to him frequently and told him of the theology of pain and the endeavour to offer up one's suffering to God. Cecilia said it strengthened her wheelchair-bound son and reinforced his spirituality. Without Enrique's constant talks, their son would never have achieved this understanding.

Enrique's own advice would soon be put into practice for himself. In 1957 he was diagnosed with incurable cancer. Enrique accepted this ordeal with Christian serenity and began a tenacious fight against the disease. It was, however, a fight he was destined to lose. He offered up his suffering for the conversion of his father, who, before Enrique's death, returned to the Church. In 1961, Argentina went through an economic crisis that led to a drop in demand for the company's glass products. The company's major shareholder in the US was going to lay off hundreds of men in Argentina. Shaw would not accept this and, ill as he was, he travelled to the US to speak with the board. He presented his case, showing them another way and told the Americans if they laid off the men, he himself would resign from the company. The board listened to his argument and decided to give him time to turn things around without implementing lay-offs among the staff. Enrique's intervention worked and the jobs of over one thousand men were saved. This was a move not forgotten by the workers. When Enrique needed blood for an operation, some two hundred factory employees turned up at the blood bank to donate their blood. Such was the love and respect they had for their managing director. After his operation, Enrique addressed the workers and tearfully thanked them for donating their blood. He told them with pride that now he had the blood of the workers coursing through his veins.

It was said of Enrique Shaw that nobody approached him without leaving better off. Such was his reputation as a fair employer and humanitarian that he came to the attention of Archbishop Jorge Mario Bergoglio, the future Pope Francis. In his capacity as Archbishop of Buenos Aires, Bergoglio began the process for Shaw's beautification. Pope Francis later said in interview with the Mexican TV station Televisa:

> I've known rich people and I'm moving forward with the cause for beatification over there in Argentina of a rich, Argentine businessman. Enrique Shaw was rich, yet saintly. A person can have money. God gives it to him so he can administer it well. And this man administered it well. Not with paternalism, but by fostering the personal growth of people who needed help.[9]

Enrique Shaw lost his battle with cancer in 1962, at the young age of forty-one. After his death, some employees approached his wife to return money Enrique had loaned them. Cecilia, in the true spirit of her beloved husband, refused to take the money, considering the loans mere donations from Enrique. Some of his employees said in interview that if other business leaders modelled their lives on Enrique, the world would be a very different place.

Enrique's life, now the subject of various studies, was Christ-centred and his business dealings were based on Catholic Social Teaching. He left little in the way of personal items, such was his detachment from the material world. An associate said of him, 'I am convinced that Shaw was a man of outstanding holiness. We'll probably have in the future the first businessman saint in the world.' This proves that the words in Mark's Gospel will never apply to Enrique Ernesto Shaw – God's businessman.

Blessed Carlo Acutis

Child of the Eucharist

Dressed in jeans, sneakers and a sweater, with a full head of dark, curly hair, the fifteen-year-old boy's appearance belied the fact that he was a saint in the making. Carlo Acutis blended in so well with his peers that only those who truly knew him realised that he was more than just an ordinary boy who loved to play football and computer games.

Born in London on 3 May 1991 to Italian parents, Carlo was baptised at the Catholic Church of Our Lady of Dolours, Fulham Road, London. The priests of that parish are delighted to claim a little of the saint in the making through his baptism at their church. Shortly after he was baptised, the family moved to Milan where

Carlo spent the rest of his young, saintly life. His mother, Antonia, said it was almost impossible for him as a child to pass a Catholic Church without going in. He loved nothing better than to stand, almost trance-like, in front of the altar. From early childhood, his conversations and questions revolved around the Church and the saints. His mother said, 'There was in him a natural predisposition for the sacred'. When he made his First Holy Communion at the age of seven, it deepened a growing spirituality that had already taken root in his tender heart and mind. It put the child on course to remain forever close to Christ. Displaying an understanding of the Mystical Body, Carlo chose to receive Holy Communion at every given opportunity. Daily Mass attendance, Eucharistic Adoration and devotion to Our Lady through the rosary quickly developed.

By the age of eleven, Carlo was helping out in his parish as a catechist. This was a position, according to his mother, that he had dearly wanted. Antonia described her son as somewhat precocious in a spiritual sense. He was able to teach the catechism, which was quite advanced for a boy of his age. He was so filled with conviction that, on every occasion, he put his head above the parapet. He would speak to his friends and classmates about the True Presence of Christ in the Tabernacle and the need to lead chaste lives. He would often encourage them to live according to Catholic moral teaching. Speaking with a maturity beyond his years, Carlo explained that the body is a gift from God and sex should be preserved for marriage. This was not an easy task for a young adolescent in a secular age of the internet, social media and smartphones. He is quoted as saying, 'If we get in front of the sun, we get a suntan, but when we get in front of the Eucharist, we become saints'.

In an interview, Carlo's mother spoke of her relationship with her son. She described it as akin to role reversal. Instead of receiving the faith from his mother, Carlo was passing it back to her and his family circle. His mother had stopped practising her religion and it was through the example of her son, who at one time considered the priesthood, that she returned to the sacraments. She spoke of an aura of authority surrounding him, which she believed came from his deep love and devotion to the Eucharist. She would consult with him and ask his advice on certain matters. Carlo brought her great comfort, especially when illness threatened to end his young life.

Antonia described Carlo as a very conscientious and thoughtful boy. He loved to be involved in charity work and often spent his own money helping those less fortunate. When other boys his age were engaging in frivolous pastimes, Carlo would often help out in the local soup kitchen in Milan and bring hot drinks and sleeping bags to the homeless, many of whom he knew by name. One particular man who was sleeping rough worried Carlo to the point where he was unable to sleep. He convinced his mother to buy a sleeping bag for the homeless man and each evening Carlo would take him freshly cooked food from his family kitchen.

A non-Christian staff member, Rajesh Mohur from Mauritius, worked for the family when Carlo was quite young. Rajesh often took him to school to the Marcelline Sisters and, on the journey home, Carlo would often ask Rajesh to take him into the church. Rajesh watched in puzzlement as the young boy stood, almost in a meditative state, in front of the tabernacle. Rajesh, a Hindu, understood none of it and asked Carlo what he was looking at. The boy explained that the Mystical Body of Christ was truly present in the Eucharist and, on each journey home, Carlo reiterated what the Real Presence meant. Rajesh was from the Brahmin caste, who specialise as priests and teachers. He explained how it is almost impossible for a Brahmin to convert, as they are the custodians of their religious traditions and customs. However, Carlo's words and deep conviction so impressed Rajesh that he began to look on Carlo as his spiritual teacher. He said Carlo's teaching transcended anything his father had ever taught him. Throughout Carlo's childhood and adolescence, Rajesh continued to learn from his young spiritual master. The necessity of the Eucharist, as explained by Carlo, for the preservation of the soul in its fight against evil, began to impact on Rajesh. He started to dream of Jesus and Mary and when he told Carlo of this, he merely replied, 'Rajesh, Jesus loves you'. In 1999, Rajesh was baptised into the Catholic Church.

Carlo also had a lighter side. He would often entertain his classmates and teachers with his infectious humour. If he could make life pleasant for those around him, he did. His Bioethics teacher, Professor Fabrizio Zaggia of the Leo XIII Institute in Milan, was honoured to have taught Carlo. He described him as being the driving force in the classroom, forming a bond of camaraderie with his fellow students. When the topic of abortion was discussed in class, the professor reported that Carlo's natural intelligence allowed him to see that life began at the moment of conception.

Described as a computer genius, Carlo was a self-taught computer programmer. When he was nine, his mother reported that he began studying computer textbooks and taught himself coding and graphic design. From age eleven, he was designing websites, not only for himself but for religious organisations, helping them to spread the Catholic faith. The internet was his way of evangelising. His own website featured cartoons for children and teenagers that taught them about the catechism.

When Carlo learned of the Eucharistic Miracles that had occurred around the world from the earliest times, he became fascinated by them. This led him to embark on one of his most impressive of projects – researching and cataloguing every Eucharistic Miracle recognised by the Church. It was the first time it had ever been done. What made the mammoth task even more impressive was that it was undertaken by a young boy. It became Carlo's mission in life to make the miracles accessible to all. Today, the Eucharistic Miracles are available at www. miracolieucaristici.org. On his personal website, available in seventeen languages and still operated by his followers, Carlo says: 'The more Eucharist we receive, the more we will become like Jesus. So that on this earth, we will have a foretaste of Heaven.' An accompanying exhibition, which displays over 150 photographs of recognised miracles, has been displayed in more than ten thousand parishes around the world.

In St John the Evangelist Church in upstate New York, the parish priest welcomed the Eucharistic exhibition. He believes that by actually seeing photos of the Eucharist changing and bleeding, it will strengthen belief. More importantly, the priest hopes it will convince the sixty per cent of non-believing Catholics that Christ is truly present in His Mystical Body. Parishioners interviewed about the exhibition spoke of their amazement and awe at the supernatural nature of the Eucharist. Many carried the experience home, as individual miracles truly impacted on them.

Carlo's second home was in Assisi, a town he loved very much as it was the birthplace of one of his favourite saints, St Francis. Young Carlo emulated St Francis. A neighbour who taught Carlo described him as a very intelligent boy with a unique simplicity. She saw in him a striking similarity to St Francis because Carlo also had a genuine concern for the homeless. One of Carlo's childhood friends, Mattia Pastorelli, remembered his extreme honesty. Discovering that he had been given twenty cent extra change when he bought an ice cream, Carlo insisted on making his friends all walk the long journey back to the ice cream parlour to return the money. He told them it would be wrong to keep it as the vendors had worked hard to make a living for their family. Christ was never far from his thoughts. Another neighbour in Assisi remembered the young Carlo interrupting his games to return home to pray.

Carlo Acutis, whose whole raison d'être had been to reunite with his Saviour, got his wish in 2006. Diagnosed with an incurable form of leukaemia when he was fifteen, the young boy praised God for giving him an alarm clock. He saw his impending death as a source of joy as he would be joining Christ in Heaven. He reassured his mother and told her not to worry, as he would give her plenty of signs of his declining health and help her to accept the inevitable. His life's plan had always been to remain close to Jesus. Many young people facing death may have felt bitter and angry at being denied a longer life. However, Carlo is quoted as saying, 'I'm happy to die because I've lived my life without wasting even a minute of it doing things that wouldn't have pleased God'. When death approached, the young boy told his mother, 'I want to offer all my suffering for the Lord, for the pope and for the Church. I don't want to do Purgatory; I want to go straight to Heaven'. It is believed by the Church that Carlo attained his goal of reaching Heaven.

Carlo's funeral in Assisi on 12 October 2006 drew mourners from every walk of life. His mother said the chapel was full of homeless people and those from Muslim and Hindu backgrounds. Such was his reputation that those who knew of him or had heard about him wanted to pay their last respects.

Father Will Conquer, a missionary priest in Cambodia, met Carlo's family and friends. He considers himself blessed to have spoken to those who knew a living saint. What impressed him most about Carlo's life is that it was an ordinary one, capable of being emulated by all. That fact alone, said Fr Will, is what gives us all hope that we too can reach for sainthood. He described Carlo as a worldwide phenomenon. His short life has inspired hundreds of social media pages, books, documentaries and YouTube videos. Carlo's influence, like the internet, is far-reaching.

Diego Olivera is a member of the Carlo Acutis Association in Argentina. He too was inspired by Carlo's online charism. Diego attests that Carlo is much loved in Latin America and throughout the world, and is seen as a friend to many. He believed the internet was Carlo's secret to continuing to evangelise, even after death.

His mother Antonia was initially perplexed by how far Carlo's fame had spread since his death. She considers it a mystery, but she believes it to be a heavenly one. She said that losing her beloved son was the most terrible thing, but she is happy that, in death, Carlo is helping people discover their faith.

What has no doubt helped Carlo's grieving family is the worldwide response from people who have informed Antonia of cures received after praying to Carlo. The cure that has elevated Carlo to Blessed is that of a young Brazilian boy, who, in 2013, was suffering from a malformed pancreas. The family prayed to Carlo to heal the boy. The Vatican investigated the case for two years before declaring the child's recovery to perfect health to be miraculous and attributable to Carlo's intervention.

When Carlo's tomb was opened in January 2019, his body had all the internal organs intact. A little work was needed to enhance his face. Carlo Acutis was beatified in the Upper Basilica of Saint Francesco in Assisi on 10 October 2020. The ceremonies lasted seventeen days and drew some three thousand people, from those who knew him to those who wanted to know him. All the churches remained open until midnight for Eucharistic Adoration and confessions were widely available. Carlo's tomb rests in the Church of Santa Maria Maggiore in Assisi. Thousands of pilgrims have visited his final resting place. People of all ages have travelled to pay their last respects and to ask for favours from the young saint in the making. What is particularly poignant is the number of young people who visit Carlo and ask for his intervention in matters that are troubling them. They see similarities between themselves and Carlo. They too love football, computer games, Pokémon – one of Carlo's favourite games – and hanging out with friends. If Carlo made it easy to reach holiness and sainthood, then hopefully a leaf can be taken out of his saintly book by many and carried home.

An apostolic letter from Pope Francis has declared that Carlo Acutis's feast will take place each year on 12 October, the anniversary of his death. Pope Francis has embraced the internet and called it a 'gift from God'. Writing to young people, he commended Carlo as being an example for his use of the internet and quoted him as saying, 'Everyone is born as an original, but many people end up dying as photocopies'. The pope added, 'Don't let that happen to you!'

Assisi, long associated with St Francis and St Clare, may be able to add another saint, Carlo Acutis, to its ranks. The city has honoured the young boy by adopting another title: The Eucharistic City. What better tribute could Assisi offer Carlo, who lived his life promoting and pleasing God, as a child of the Eucharist?

Conclusion

It is hoped that the stories of the remarkable lives of these men and women will be a source of encouragement to many. Their unbelievable courage and unshakable faith, even in the face of death, has marked many of them out for sainthood. Their backgrounds and experiences were as diverse as their callings. They came from farms and mansions, from near and far, to dedicate their lives, works and sufferings to Almighty God. Child, adult, student, teacher, religious and laity, all took up their cross and left an indelible mark on the world. These men and women are a prime example of how ordinary people can make extraordinary things happen and can change countless lives.

Endnotes

1   Kevin Madigan, 'Madigan on Cornwell, *Hitler's Pope: The Secret History of Pius XII*', H-Holocaust, April 2000, networks.h-net. org/node/6088/reviews/7219/madigan-cornwell-hitlers-pope-secret-history-pius-xii; accessed 10 September 2021.

2   Israel Zolli, *Before the Dawn* (San Francisco: Ignatius Press, 2008), p. 195.

3   Richard Armstrong, *Out to Change the World: A Life of Father James Keller of The Christophers* (New York: Crossroads Publishing Company, 1984).

4   Brian Fleming, *The Vatican Pimpernel: The Wartime Exploits of Monsignor Hugh O'Flaherty* (Cork: The Collins Press, 2008).

5   James Patrick Derum, *The Porter of Saint Bonaventure's: The Life of Father Solanus Casey, Capuchin* (Texas: Fidelity Press, 1968).

6   Barbara Tepa Lupack, 'Two Aspects of Auschwitz: Violence and Charity', from *The Polish Review*, Vol. 28, No. 2 (Illinois: University of Illinois Press, 1983), pp. 88–97.

7   The events in this story are based on the diary of Fr Bishop SJ, which were published in the book *Possessed: The True Story of an Exorcism* by Thomas B. Allen. Father Walter Halloran SJ approved the manuscript of the book and both he and Fr Bowdern SJ, the chief exorcist, confirmed the events were accurate.

8   Raymond Arroyo, *Mother Angelica: The Remarkable Story of a Nun, Her Nerve and a Network of Miracles* (New York: Crown Publishing Group, 2007).

9   'Enrique Shaw: the Argentine businessman whom Francis may soon beatify', *Catholic News Agency*, 3 August 2015, www. catholicnewsagency.com/news/32417/enriqueshaw; accessed 18 September 2021.